peace love and lemonade:

a recipe to make your life sweeter

Created and Written by
Nancy Stampahar

First Edition

Peace, Love and Lemonade®:
A Recipe to Make Your Life Sweeter

Nancy Stampahar

Printed in the United States of America.

ISBN: 978-0-9800927-0-7
Library of Congress Control Number: 2007940102

Published by Silver Lining Solutions™

Printing Services Provided by:
Business Alternatives, Inc.
630 Plum Indusrial Court
Pittsburgh, Pennsylvania 15239

This book is dedicated to my mother,
Carol, whom I love and admire
for having the courage to make a better life
for herself and her children;
and to my very gentle brother, Jeff,
whom I called "Bro" and deeply loved.
His spirit will live within me forever,
and I will always remember him.

TABLE OF CONTENTS

To laugh often and much; to win the respect of intelligent people and the affection of children; to earn the appreciation of honest critics and endure the betrayal of false friends; to appreciate beauty; to find the best in others; to leave the world a bit better whether by a healthy child, a garden patch or a redeemed social condition; to know even one life has breathed easier because you have lived.

This is to have succeeded.

-- Ralph Waldo Emerson

INTRODUCTION

I was born into inspiration. In 1963, when I was two years old, my mother decided to divorce her abusive husband after five years of marriage. In retaliation for this courageous act, my mother, my four-year-old intellectually-disabled brother and I were locked out of our row house, with some of our belongings scattered out on the lawn. That day, the lives of my family of three changed forever.

As my childhood evolved, I had a very difficult time feeling good about life, and more importantly, feeling good about myself. I felt damaged and thought that I was not worthy of having a good life. I could not cope with my hardships of being poor and living in a single-parent house with a "different" and limited sibling. When I was in my vulnerable teens, at the age of thirteen, I escaped my stress and pain with excessive partying, which included drugs and alcohol. First, I dropped out of life. Then, I dropped out of high school.

As my young adult life evolved into adulthood, I took steps forward and backward until I came into this great place of happiness and fulfillment. The steps I took represented the choices I made; some were wise and some were not. I eventually earned my college degree in human resource management and created my own organizational training and keynote speaking business to empower people to improve their work performances and live great lives. I learned firsthand how to go from nowhere to somewhere by watching my family's ability to triumph over tough circumstances. I learned the power of choice. I learned how to make lemonade out of lemons.

Life is hard for everyone some of the time. At times, we all experience the sour, bitter taste of lemons. How we react to each tough experience, however, is a choice we can make--not one that others make for us. We can either choose to face the challenges we encounter and take control of our situations or we can wallow in them and let life and work difficulties direct us.

Are you embracing life and fully living or are you waking up each day just existing in this world? Do you like how you are living your life? Do you keep finding reasons for not doing what you really want to do? What takes up your time and drains your energy, making you exhausted and miserable? What causes you undue stress, physical ailments or accidents? What needs to be fixed in your life? What is making you lose who you are and what you want in your life? What are you dealing with in your life that you just can't take anymore? Who is taking you for granted or taking advantage of you? Why are you letting them? What will it take to make you want to do something differently to live a happy and fulfilling life?

Many people in our society are not truly happy and not living the life they deeply desire. In today's fast-paced, multi-tasking society, many people are not getting involved in living.

They are choosing the path of least resistance, which leaves them complacent and stuck. They keep responding to situations in the same ways, and keep getting the same results. People can let themselves go or never find their power of choice.

Perhaps you feel that you simply exist in this world by going through the motions and not questioning who you are, how you became who you are, and more importantly, how you *could* be. Even when you face hardships and overwhelming circumstances, you can make peace with your past, instill love within yourself and create lemonade for your future. This book will show you how.

No matter how tough our lives have been, we can reach "our greatness potential." It is deep inside us. For some people it is easy to find; others have to try a little harder. By trying, we find courage to move beyond our comfort zones. Our courage helps us to become more assertive, to ask for what we want and need, and to discover our unique passions. When we find courage, assertiveness and passion, we have found our greatness potential.

As a result of my family's ability to triumph over tough circumstances, I have chosen the trite yet powerful phrase: "When life hands you lemons, make lemonade," as the primary theme through this book. "Lemons" are commonly referred to metaphorically as unpleasant, tough experiences that can make life difficult to enjoy and manage. They can come from some typical parts of life, or from extenuating circumstances and extreme hardships. You make lemonade by squeezing the lemons, removing the seeds, grating the zest and adding sugar. When you choose to make lemonade from these metaphoric lemons, you decide to do something positive as a reaction to your unfortunate circumstance. Choosing to make lemonade will help you change your perspectives and behaviors, so that good things can happen for you.

While some people choose to make lemonade, some remain bitter. It's easier to take the path of least resistance; it's simpler and faster not to think and question, not to ask for help and not to deal with our situations and feelings. When we choose not to make our lives better, we are also choosing not to take responsibility for our own happiness. On the flipside, when we choose to make our lives better, we are choosing to do something positive and productive to bring happiness and fulfillment to our lives. It's a matter of choice.

The lemons themselves do not influence a situation as much as the lemons' seeds and their skin. You will discover that the lemon's seeds are the emotions of anger, fear, guilt and shame. These seeds need to be removed because they are taking up too much room, time and energy. They take away our power and shift our focus. They can cause us to think, say and do things we did not intend. They can keep us from living the life, working the work and having the relationships we deserve and deeply desire.

The skin of every lemon contains something wonderful that gets us through tough times. The skin holds the lighthearted zest, which brings us positive energy. It should be grated off our lemons. We need it to bring fresh flavor to our lives and keep things light every once in a while. The lemon's zest helps us smile, laugh, act playful and have fun. How aware or unaware we are of our own lemon's seeds and zest greatly affects our ability to make peace, love and lemonade. Even in times of heartache and tragedy, lemons teach us the lessons necessary to grow and become happier people.

I created a lemonade recipe to make your life sweeter. It will help you with the "how to" once you decide you are ready. In a straightforward, organized process, it will show you what to do when you "can't take it anymore." It can bring you positive results if you continuously try and commit to give it your best. The self-development process will help you discover your greatness potential to live a happier and more fulfilling life. In return, you will have to make a lifetime commitment to adapt your thoughts, feelings and behaviors when you encounter tough times. You are the one person who is responsible for your life.

Through true stories and examples from my life and

You are the one person who is responsible for your life.

reflections on your own life, you will discover practical techniques and wisdom to overcome the obstacles you encounter in your life and work. You will come to see that the same basic principles and applications can be used both at work and at home. You will gain a keen awareness and understanding of some effective life skills and character traits that can be applied in both your professional and personal lives. These life skills and character traits shape our behaviors. They are the foundation for success and happiness. You will feel inspired when you realize that in our own way, in our own time, my family of three discovered how to make our lives better. You will feel pride once you begin to make your own life better in your own way and in your own time.

The self-reflection questions and worksheets throughout this book will give you the opportunity to see, through your own writing, how you are living, working and being in this world, and more importantly how you *could* live, work and be in this world. You will gain the most benefit when you make a commitment to yourself to complete the worksheets and stay focused on *your own personal growth.* The reading, writing and reflecting necessary for your happiness will take some soul-searching that might make you cry tears of triumph and disappointment. When you choose to do something different and unfamiliar, you must accept that it is not going to be easy. If you want an easy, magical solution, this book is not for you. It will require mental and emotional time and energy.

If you want some things in your life to be different, this book is for you. Personal growth is ongoing. The process will require you to say and do things differently. You may feel afraid or awkward. This is normal and okay when you are trying to change how you act and react towards people and situations. If you cry as you move through this book, notice what makes you cry sad tears and happy tears. Tears represent truths. To bring genuine happiness into your life, you must discover your own truths.

Oh, and lighten it up once in a while by remembering to laugh at yourself, and at me too. That's why the zest is on lemons. It brings enjoyment and reduces stress. Once you begin to know who you are and what you want in both your personal life and your professional life, you will find authentic happiness and fulfillment.

Once you decide to make lemonade from your lemons, you will become more open to pinpointing your unique lemons, your lemons' seeds, and their zest. This is the great beginning. Then, you can begin to stir up your greatness potential

When you make something positive out of negative, tragic, or painful circumstances, you can more easily deal with them.

sweeteners of courage, assertiveness and passion. Finally, you must blend in the main ingredients to make your best lemonade ever. They are: one-third cup accountability, one-third cup attitude and one-third cup action. This full cup of ingredients will create your strategies and action plans for improved results. They will help you achieve your own desired outcomes and goals. You must set goals if you want to make lemonade out of your lemons. You must set goals and take action on them if you want positive results. You must follow through and make wise choices.

In this brief read, you will connect in varying degrees with the circumstances and the reactions that affect many people when tough times occur. You will see through my real-life success and failure stories how powerful choices are. The most important message of this book is that when tough times come your way, the way you react to them will have a tremendous impact on how sweet or sour your life will be. When you make something positive out of negative, tragic, or painful circumstances, you can more easily deal with them. My mother had a choice: to stay complacent and stay on welfare, or to make something of herself and her life. I'm glad she chose the latter because she became a great role model with her career-focused determination. It became ingrained in me that people have to work hard for what they want, especially if they don't want to settle for less than they deserve. I learned that I must never give up when I am struggling to achieve my goals because the rewards will be better than the unhappiness and pain. I made a choice to drop out of high school, which did not follow the path of my role model. When I made a choice to drop back into high school, I proudly realized that I inherited some great traits from my mother. Over the years, I have learned how to keep making good things happen--not only in my life, but also in the lives of others. I am empowered to live; but more importantly, I am empowered to do what it takes to live the life I truly want. If you want to make yourself more happy and your life better, get ready; you're about to discover how to make some sweet lemonade!

How to Make Your Life Sweeter

Choose to Make Lemonade
Gather Your Lemons
Remove Your Lemons' Seeds and Grate Off the Lighthearted Zest

Stir Up Your Greatness Potential Sweeteners of:
Courage
Assertiveness
Passion

Blend in the Lemonade Ingredients of:
1/3 Cup Accountability
1/3 Cup Attitude
1/3 Cup Action
Sip Your Lemonade Slowly and Enjoy Your Sweeter Life!

INTRODUCTION:
SELF REFLECTION QUESTIONS

If you connect with any of the following questions, you must decide whether you want to make yourself happier and your life more fulfilling. If your answers to the following questions are mostly "yes" or "often," it's time to consider making some positive changes in your life. Remember, you have the power to make choices for yourself. You have the power to live a great life. You can choose to make lemonade.

How often do I catch myself saying, "I don't have time to deal with this!" or "I just can't take it anymore!"?

Have I "let myself go," in that I no longer take care of myself physically, mentally or emotionally?

Do I stay in my comfort zone and resist change?

Do I tend to have perfectionist, people-pleasing tendencies?

Do I carry grudges and have a difficult time forgiving others, as well as myself?

Do I let people take advantage of me?

Am I so afraid of conflict that I do not express how I honestly feel and what I want to see happen?

Do I find it challenging to give myself some "me-time"?

Have I lost my passion?

Do I think that I may never have found my passion?

CHAPTER 1: LOST IN LIFE

There was a time when I was so lost that I kept choosing to let life take me down. Life was hard. I wasn't ready to be happy. I didn't think I was worthy to live a sweeter life. When I hit those rebellious teenage years, I rebelled with a vengeance. I was very dysfunctional, at-risk and unhealthy. I couldn't deal with life. I was out of control because I hated myself, my life and all my family circumstances. I decided not to cope with my tough times. I did not make wise choices.

I chose to use excessive alcohol and drugs to escape my pain and anger. Alcohol, coke, speed and pot were my drugs of choice--not lemonade. I began polluting my body eight years before legally permitted. During eighth grade I had my first experiences with marijuana and cigarettes. I eventually became a pack-a-day smoker, until partying days and nights led me to be a two-pack-a-day smoker. I didn't care about what I was doing to my body and my life. I was not making peace, love and lemonade.

I had no ambition or motivation, because I had no self-esteem. I hated school from eighth grade on. My grades and attendance steadily declined. When I was in the tenth grade, my second semester report card showed that I had failed four out of eight classes, and I had withdrawn from the remaining four. What a failure I was. School was boring and my priority was partying. I just did not fit into school. Oh, the dread that would fill me when a teacher called upon me to speak up in front of other students. I hated those in-the-spotlight moments because of how incompetent I felt.

By the time I was in the eleventh grade, I thought I knew everything I needed to know. I was such a rebellious teenager that when I decided I didn't want to go to high school anymore, I just quit. I dropped out. I had many quiet days while everyone I knew was either in school or working-- everyone but my senile grandmother, Nanny, who was struggling with growing old and lonely. Each day, Nanny and I faced our individual struggles.

During the summer months between eleventh and twelfth grades, my friends were talking about becoming seniors and graduating. Some were even making plans to attend college. During this time, one of my ah-ha light bulbs went on, telling me that graduating from high school is important, a necessity in life. Through many discussions, a wonderful guidance counselor championed me, essentially telling the administration that I was a bright kid who just needed a structured learning environment and some attention. My lemons were piling up and she wanted to help me make lemonade.

Because I caused so much aggravation in my high school with my truancy, failing grades, lies, and getting caught smoking pot in the third floor girl's bathroom, the administration gave me a hard time about classroom placement. Thanks to my guidance counselor, I was placed in AIC, Adaptive Instructional Class, for my senior year of high school. This class of about ten students was for troubled, at-risk teens. Yes, troubled and lost I was. This class was for students just like me. I did not have any learning disabilities; I had disciplining and feeling-good-about-myself disabilities. I still was into partying, but at least I finally was willing to focus on my studies. The structured environment was exactly what I needed to excel. It gave me a sense of belonging and the attention I so desperately needed. I chose to make lemonade by going back to school.

Students rarely return to school after dropping out, but my high school decided to graduate me on time because of my determination, extra efforts and significant grade and attendance improvements. By then, I realized that when we are finally open-minded and ready to do something different, to have something different, we can. Woohoo--I graduated from high school!

This significant life experience helped me decide that instead of taking my unhappiness out on myself and everyone around me, I'd make the most of my circumstances by choosing to do things that would make me happy. I needed to

> **Once you discover what you really value and want in your life, you can begin making choices that are aligned with your values, wants and desires.**

make changes within myself. I realized that if I make myself happy first, I can make others happy too.

The more you understand yourself and the many facets of your life, the more you can grow to enjoy the people and situations that surround you. Once you discover what you really value and want in your life, you can begin making choices that are aligned with your values, wants and desires. Many people never make the time to reflect upon who they are, how they are living and what they want in life. Many know only what they *don't* want in their lives, instead of what they *do* want in their lives. They just accept things as they are, without realizing that there are many other ways of living and being.

I discovered that while I am alive I have the power to choose the directions I want to go in this world. I learned that I cannot wait for happiness to come my way; I have to go find happiness. I found that I could be happy by deciding to live my life differently and reacting positively to the toughest circumstances. And guess what? I didn't have to go far because that place of happiness was already within me; it just got lost. Through my own journey from surviving, to existing, to celebrating my family, I have come full circle to a wonderful place of awareness, authenticity, fulfillment and happiness.

Even with all the growth and empowerment I live by now, I am not a perfect human being who never makes a wrong decision, says the wrong thing, gets down, or feels fears or insecurities. I do. If you ever saw me sing karaoke, dance the two-step, work with technology or become nervous, hurt, or scared, you surely would see that I have limitations just as all human beings do. I've just learned to accept myself, with my positive traits, my flaws, and my mistakes. I now know how to take care of myself to get back up when life gets me down.

If you never experience tough circumstances in your life, you will be fortunate not to feel the pain and frustration that come with them. On the flipside, you will not deeply understand how precious life is and how much happier you can be when you embrace its opportunities and the people you encounter. Through your experiences, you learn life's lessons, adopt beliefs and values, and gain wisdom. By reflecting positively on your experiences, your inner voice will develop the positive thinking which will make you happier. This is how you must deal with life. This is how you make lemonade.

If I wanted to continue wallowing in my tough circumstances by hating myself and not returning to high school, where would I be now? I'll never know, but there's a good chance that without a high school degree, I would either be living on welfare or earning a low income. I would likely have a drug and alcohol problem with no real purpose in or gratitude for life. Wherever I would be, I'm sure I would not be as happy a person as I am. Had I not chosen to live a better, healthier life, I would have stayed stay stuck, without any confidence and hope. On that summer day when I was a high school dropout, I began feeling thirsty for happiness. I quenched my thirst with my first refreshingly sweet glass of lemonade. Boy, was it sweet!

CHAPTER 1:
SELF REFLECTION QUESTIONS

The following questions reflect the messages in this chapter. Answering them honestly will give you a greater understanding of how effectively you cope and how well you know yourself. You must decide whether you want to make yourself happier and your life more fulfilling. If you realize that you do not cope well during tough times and do not know yourself too well, it's time to consider making some positive changes in your life. Remember, you have the power to make choices for yourself. You have the power to live a great life. You can choose to make lemonade.

How do I cope? What stress management techniques do I use?

What do I value? What is *most* important to me in the areas of: career, family, finances, intellectual activities, physical activities, relationships, social activities or spirituality? What else is important to me?

What lessons have I learned and what wisdom have I gained? Answer the question: if I knew then, what I know now, what would I do differently?

CHAPTER 2:
WHAT ARE LEMONS?

Lemons are the tough circumstances people encounter. Some are typical parts of life, and some arise from extenuating circumstances or extreme hardships. Some of the frustrating times we experience are self-induced and some come from circumstances beyond our control. While we have the power to help reduce the number of challenging experiences, it is not possible to live a lemon-free life. Life and people are not perfect. They are complex. We can get our greatest heartaches and frustrations from life and people. Yet, we can get our greatest joys from life and people.

Calculated risk-taking is necessary to live a happy and fulfilling life.

Most people do not like lemons because they can bring stress and heartache. Lemons can temporarily take away our happy times and make them challenging. Some people avoid making choices that could bring them greater happiness and fulfillment because of the hard work and risk involved. They avoid making lemonade and taking risks in order to keep mistakes and frustrations out of their lives. When this happens, they are choosing to let their lemons leave a lingering sour taste in their lives. They are staying stuck with the status quo. Anything worthwhile involves taking calculated risks, which can bring out our fears and increase our stress levels. Calculated risk-taking is necessary to live a happy peace love and lemonade

and fulfilling life. Making lemonade out of lemons is a choice.

Life is unpredictable. It changes rapidly. Our lives can become exhausting from all the chaos and heartache of tough times. Sometimes we find ourselves mourning the loss of loved ones, jobs, or pleasurable activities. Especially when we are courageously taking risks and experiencing learning curves, an openness to life and feelings can make challenging circumstances feel overwhelming. When we experience tough times, all seems wrong. Once we begin to approach our circumstances in a positive light, we will realize that our hard times are necessary to help us grow and evolve to be better people.

Are you one of those people who keeps doing the same things and keep getting the same unfortunate results in your personal or professional life? I was one of those people--the kind of person who was not happy, the kind of person who did not "get" what I needed to relieve my stress and chaos. I could not see through all the overwhelming circumstances. I could not commit to taking care of myself. I could not see how necessary my lemons were to bring about my sweeter way of living today.

Perhaps all your negative energy from your tough times has squelched your desire and confidence. You may no longer enjoy the work you do, the people in your life and the activities that once brought excitement and fun. You may no longer appreciate your loved ones and yourself--or even being alive. Your lack of desire and drive are making you settle for less than you deserve.

Some people truly believe they are happy and living the best life they can. They honestly have no idea what they have been missing because they have never been exposed to any other way of living. That is, until someone or some new experience shows them differently. Quite often, you do not realize how badly you feel until you actually begin feeling better. If you open yourself to learning and discovering different ways of living and being, you will realize that your life can be better than it currently is. If you stay cocooned and continue to perceive life and your circumstances with a closed mind, nothing will get better. There will always be a "black cloud" hanging over you, waiting to descend.

We live our lives by the ways we think. When you accept things as they are and do not question yourself and your tough circumstances, you will not grow. You limit yourself. You need to think positively and curiously if you want to fulfill your desire to be happy, loved and accepted. You can let go of your past disappointments and move toward a happier future. While you may know all of these points intellectually, you may not fully connect your knowledge with the emotions of your heart. Your heart and mind must come together for you to take action.

> **Success is uniquely defined by each individual according to his or her strengths, interests and happiness.**

When the connection happens, you finally "get it."

Oh, the pressure and pride of an intelligent, determined family. My extended family members were people of great intelligence and some found their drive to succeed from rags to riches. These great role models showed me that no matter how poor someone is, anyone can succeed and reach his or her greatness potential. Success is not necessarily defined by earning a college degree and a high income. Success is uniquely defined by each individual according to his or her strengths, interests and happiness. To me, success is not how much money someone has. It is how much character someone has. When people treat themselves and others with respect, they have succeeded. When people make choices for their lives to better themselves and others, they have succeeded.

I had it in my mind that someday I could be like the intelligent, determined people in my family. I did not have it in my heart. I knew intellectually that it was possible to achieve a good education and a career simply because people do. But deep down, I did not believe that I, Nancy Jean Stampahar, was smart enough to achieve a good life or--more importantly--

deserving of one. I kept too many negative thoughts and emotions within me. When you carry negative thoughts and emotions within you, you empower frustrating circumstances to occur. Negative thinking and emotions create opportunities for you to bring about your own self-induced frustrating circumstances. When you are able to evolve your negative thoughts and emotions into positive thinking and reactions, good things will happen in your life. You will begin making peace, love and lemonade.

> When you carry negative thoughts and emotions within you, you empower frustrating circumstances to occur.

After two years of struggling in the college scene, I failed once again and flunked out of my second year. The first year I had gone to a local community college because I had not taken the required SAT tests. My grades were average. The second year I wanted to go away to college, but I was declined admission. Like my mother, I put my determination into action. I drove one and a half hours to speak directly with a dean. While I do not recall much of our conversation, I'm sure my strong determination prevailed, and I was admitted. Well, I did win that battle but I still was irresponsible and troubled. I just wasn't ready to be happy. I flunked out with a failing cumulative GPA. I went to work instead of school.

After a few years, I realized that I wanted a professional career. I had to try again. I attended a local business school, and earned a certificate in travel and tourism. I made a wise choice and began to excel into a professional career.

It took me over ten years to say to myself, "I need a college education if I am going to have a successful career." I wanted it. *I was thirsty, and I decided to make my life sweeter.* As a result, I finally graduated from Robert Morris University at age thirty-five. Woohoo! The phrase "better late than never" proved true. I can still feel the pride and joy I experienced the last day I drove around the college building. I thought to myself, "Wow, guess I am smart." In the end I had not failed at school, and I was on my way to a wonderful career path and a better life. I was building the confidence that comes from first trying and then achieving something I really wanted. Earning my college degree was like making sweet lemonade.

My educational lemons kept me feeling incompetent. I could not get myself to make lemonade for many years. When I tried, I failed. I wasn't ready--yet. We must be ready to make something of ourselves and our lives. We must be ready to make peace, love and lemonade. If not, we will fail, and perhaps give up completely. What will it take for you to be ready?

WHICH WOULD YOU PREFER?

Gathering My Lemons Worksheet

Use the following questions to begin the process of gathering your lemons. Go back in your memory and think of the tough times you have encountered in your personal and professional life. Or, you can think about a tough time you are currently experiencing. Now, just select one lemon that you are ready to make into lemonade. That will be the lemon to gather. As you move through this book, you will continue to reflect on this experience that has affected your life. Then, *you* must decide whether you want to overcome your challenge and make lemonade.

CHAPTER 2:
GATHERING MY LEMONS WORKSHEET

Gathering My Lemons	My Lemon Reflections
What lemons have I experienced in my life?	
Which lemon is still bringing me difficulties?	
Which one will I gather?	
At the time when I got handed this lemon, why did I think it happened?	
What impact did the difficult experience have on me and those who were involved?	
Reflecting back, now, why do I think I was handed this lemon and what did I learn from this tough time?	

CHAPTER 2:
SELF REFLECTION QUESTIONS

The following questions reflect the messages in this chapter. Answer them honestly and decide whether you want to make yourself happier and your life more fulfilling. If your answers to the following questions are mostly "yes" or "often," it's time to consider making some positive changes in your life. Remember, you have the power to make choices for yourself. You have the power to live a great life. You can choose to make lemonade.

Do I avoid taking risks because of the hard work and fear involved?

Am I closed-minded to learning and discovering different ways of living and being?

Am I knowledgeable on how to best take care of myself but do not apply my knowledge?

Deep down, do I believe I am *not* deserving of a better life?

Do I keep saying to myself that I want to do something about my situations but do not follow through?

CHAPTER 3:
LEMON SEEDS AND LIGHTHEARTED ZEST

The seeds in our lemons carry our emotions of anger, fear, guilt and shame. The zest of our lemons carries our lightheartedness. Our seeds and zest bring us decreased or increased energy, affecting our daily lives and our reactions to situations. Our emotions have a tremendous impact on our responses to people and situations. If we choose to let our emotions fester inside us, we will not find peace; we will not find happiness. Our festering emotions will affect our daily living and spirit. While dealing with our emotions can be overwhelming, exhausting and time consuming, we need to remove our lemon's seeds by making wise choices. When we need to lighten up some of our intense, heavy moments, we can grate off some of our lemon's lighthearted zest to find some relief.

Here is an example of how I received a fear seed and how I had removed it. When I was in the seventh grade, I was attacked and bitten by a German shepherd-collie dog while delivering the local newspaper after school. I felt excruciating physical pain from the dog attack in both my legs and lost a favorite pair of pants. To this day, I can vividly see my horrific experience. I mostly remember not the pain in my legs, but how disappointed I was when my really groovy, one-of-a-kind pants were mutilated and could never be worn again. Darn. They were of soft, suede-like material, tie-dyed in shades of brown and tan. That was a real bummer because I really, really

loved those cool pants.   The pain went away after a few days, but it took years for me to stop being afraid of dogs when they were near me. Fear of dogs was instilled in me that day.
Until I was exposed to more gentle dogs like golden retrievers, I remained afraid. Exposure to golden retrievers helped me to realize that not all dogs are mean and out to attack me. My new experiences with kind, friendly dogs finally allowed me to remove the fear seed from that traumatic experience.

As silly as it may seem to be upset about losing a pair of pants, those pants were extremely precious and worth millions of dollars to me since we were a low-income family living in a mid-to-upper-class community. They had made me feel "cool" like the rich kids. At that time, I could only see losing those pants as a negative experience because I might not be "cool" without them. Now, I can see that even when I no longer had those pants, I did get a better education and exposure to "the good life." I learned about a higher quality of living and what money can and cannot buy. I now believe that being poor in an affluent community was actually a good thing. I changed the way I thought about the experience. I made lemonade.

My aunt used to call me a hydraulic because I kept pushing my emotions down so tightly that they couldn't get released. When I was growing up, my family did not talk about feelings and our "stuff," although at one point, my mother did try to

You will seek help only when you are strong enough to admit that you're making unhealthy choice, and you are ready to start making healthy choices.

get me to talk with a counselor. Bless her heart for trying. The two times I went to the counselor's office, I did not want any help. I wanted to pretend like everything was okay so I would not have to go to counseling anymore. According to my mother, the counselor said I was fine. I'm sure my misleading of the counselor was because I couldn't admit that anything was wrong with me and my life. Mostly, I didn't want to feel and deal. I wasn't ready.

You will seek help only when you are strong enough to admit that you're making unhealthy choices, and you are ready to start making healthy choices. Your negative thoughts and emotions can stay inside you for too long and guide you in the wrong directions. You must dig inside your tough times a little deeper to determine what kind of seeds your lemons hold. You need to determine which emotions--anger, fear, guilt or shame--have been affecting your life. Your lemons may only have one or two kinds of seeds or may have all four.

Every lemon has some lighthearted zest on it. The zest can lift you up, and make living easier and more fun. To make your life happier and more gratifying, you must remove your seeds and occasionally grate off some zest. Deciding to remove your seeds and grate some zest is done by choice--your choice.

I was thirty-four years old when I finally decided to begin the process of removing my seeds out of my lemons. When I

Every lemon has some lighthearted zest on it.

moved back home after being away for many years, all my life hardships finally caught up with me. Between the years of excessive partying and being away from my tough circumstances, I had escaped having to deal with my pain and heartache. Then, shazam! My past experiences came back with a vengeance. At first, I didn't realize what was happening to me. I had bouts of dizziness, heart palpitations, numbness and shortness of breath. I went to my doctor on numerous occasions to be tested for disorders like ischemia, lupus and multiple sclerosis. I even walked around with a heart monitor on a couple of separate occasions. My body was doing all of these foreign things, which scared me. I thought I must have some sort of disease. Fortunately, I did not.

The only thing wrong with my body was that my big ole' heart had been broken too many times at such a young age. My broken heart caused me anxiety and worry. My childhood experiences had finally caught up with me. I was having panic  attacks from the stress of all the emotions that were surfacing after having been pushed down within me for many years. My emotions were being expressed physically, instead of verbally. I had many suppressed feelings that I did not know how to express. Even worse, I couldn't specifically identify what I was feeling. I just knew that I did not feel good, and I wanted to feel better. So, I finally began to make my own lemonade by going to therapy. I found an excellent therapist to help me deal with the same stuff I should have dealt with seventeen years earlier. As they say, "Better late than never."

It's never too late to get happy. It's never too late to make our lives better. I spent a few years in therapy dealing with the painful emotions I had experienced. It was a pivotal moment when my therapist said, "You have to if you want to feel better." That was the moment I chose to make a commitment to taking care of myself. I really didn't have a choice for this situation--there were no alternatives. I had to start dealing with my emotions and baggage. I found my strong desire and determination for self-discovery healing. My process also included self-directed education through self-help books, articles and seminars. During this time, I was taking a Human Resource Management college course entitled, "Psychology of Adjustment," which was in perfect timing with my personal transformation. Through a lot of hard work, I finally found peace. The panic attacks never returned and neither has the heavy use of drugs and alcohol. Therapy, self-help homework and my personal desire to be happy and healthy really were the only ways I could heal from my past.

Everyone can use a good dose of therapy or self-development activities in his or her life because everyone has lemons and every lemon has seeds. Unfortunately, many people hold varied negative perceptions about therapy. They may feel ashamed because they think it's only for "crazy" people, and they sure wouldn't want others to think they are crazy. They might believe that asking for help is a sign of weakness, when doing so is actually a sign of strength, courage and self-respect. They may be afraid of what they might discover and feel from their therapy, which is why many people stop going after a session or two. Finally, they may have heard negative stories about therapists. In any profession, there are those who are good and those who are bad at what they do. If you decide to seek a therapist, you need to take a proactive approach to finding one who best fits your needs and personality. You must put in the time, effort and energy that's necessary to achieve positive results from therapy. If you're not willing to make a commitment to yourself and do the deep "squeezing" that is necessary to make yourself feel better, chances are that therapy and books like this won't help you.

After my first session, I came home and wrote the simple poem on the following page to myself to carry me through the process.

I SEE YOUR SAD TEARS
I SEE YOUR PAIN

I BELIEVE YOUR BEAUTIFUL EYES
SHOULD NO LONGER BE DISGUISED

I KNOW YOU'RE STRONG
I KNOW YOU'RE BRAVE

IT COULD TAKE DAYS
IT COULD TAKE YEARS

BUT SOMEDAY, I KNOW
YOU WILL CRY HAPPY TEARS.

May-June, 1995

I finally cry happy tears. Personal growth in therapy is an ongoing and private process, but I learned that when we share our hardships and how we overcame them with others, we can help them not to feel so alone, damaged and inadequate. When we give others hope and inspiration to make their lives better, we can remember and feel proud that we overcame too.

Our tough times can be very frustrating and painful when we are going through them. They can leave us full of negative thoughts and emotions, which can be very frightening and overwhelming. When we respond positively to our circumstances, thoughts and emotions, we can find happiness, and make our lives and the lives of others better. To deal with and express our thoughts and emotions is a difficult choice, especially at first, but ultimately, a wise choice.

Anger	Have respect for other people
Fear	Focus on positive outcomes
Guilt	Live without regrets
Shame	Realize that you are deserving

| Lighthearted Zest -- SMILE, LAUGH, AND HAVE FUN |

THE ANGER SEED

Every survivor knows both the power of and the need for anger. It moves us to act and react. It forces us to do what is necessary to get our needs met and to survive. It's certainly an emotion felt by a woman fleeing from an abusive husband with two infants in her arms, trying to safeguard her children. This determined and angry woman was my mother, and my brother and I were the two infants in her arms, with no money and no place to call home.

Sometimes our mother's anger scared us and made us feel bad about ourselves as we grew up. We were young and impressionable, and these were normal reactions to anger. As youngsters, we didn't understand why Mommy was mad. Today, I understand it. Although some of my mother's anger spilled over onto us, most of it was directed toward productive activities. My mother needed her anger to keep us fed and clothed, and to protect us. It made her do positive things with her life. It pushed her to succeed. She needed anger to protect her hurting heart and soul. Anger made her feel in control. Anger made her take control of her life. Anger made her want to prove to herself that she could do whatever it took to have a better life for herself and her children. That's healthy anger. It makes good things happen for good people. When we use our anger to energize and fuel us into doing something positive and productive for ourselves and others, we make our lives better.

More wonderfully, we make the lives of others better, too.

With the passing of my wonderful brother, I experienced my saddest lemon, my biggest heartache. I always knew that my brother's death was going to be the most difficult experience I would face, no matter how long I lived, because I never fully dealt with the heartfelt emotions that come from loving and living with someone who has limitations. I let my emotions fester deep inside me. I knew the hardships he had experienced on his own and the ones we went through together would eventually surface when I grieved his death.

Ever since we were toddlers, we experienced how mean some people, even kids, can be. One afternoon when Jeff and I were in our late thirties, I asked him, "What do you remember from when we were kids?" He replied, "Getting hit on the head with a brick." I remembered that too because I was there. We were playing under cement steps, alongside a city street, when a standard-sized brick smacked against my brother's head. We were scared. He hurt inside and out. As I had on many occasions, I grabbed his hand and we ran home to be safe from the cruelty of others. Scenes like this made us believe we were unwanted, unliked, and damaged--especially Jeff. Heartbreaking stories of people being mean, rude and cruel toward my brother have always been too painful to discuss. To see someone I loved being harmed, ridiculed and continuously excluded breaks my heart. I would feel both angry and sad for my brother when people did not have compassion and were unkind, disrespectful, or mean to my gentle "Bro." I was also angry at myself for not speaking up and lashing out at them for hurting my brother. I've since been told that I did the right thing by walking away instead of fighting fire with fire. It's better to walk away when we are angry than express to our anger in unhealthy ways. It's the better person who is kind, compassionate and respectful toward all people.

We notice unhealthy anger in people who are being aggressive, rude, inflexible and closed-minded. They take their anger out on others, usually those most near and dear. This kind of aggression is not an effective way to cope with anger. It is disrespectful and hurtful to those who receive the brunt of it.

Another unhealthy coping mechanism is excessive use of drugs and alcohol. This was my coping method of choice during my rebellious teenage years. The much heavier use began the summer going into ninth grade, when I met a new set of friends during a time when I was most vulnerable and angry. I was vulnerable because I was lost and on the run to escape my tough circumstances.

That same summer, I was trying out for the high school tennis team. I remember one day running into my new friends

> **No matter how difficult a situation may be, you must choose to make lifetime fixes if you want a better life.**

who were going to the America mellow rock concert. I had tennis team tryouts and could not go. We went our separate ways that day. They went to party and have fun. I went to experience another disappointment. I lost my tennis match and was eliminated from the team's tryouts. I didn't make the team. That day, I *decided* to give up trying. I joined the party team instead because I couldn't risk facing another disappointment in my life. I took the easy way out of life. I chose not to make lemonade. This is not the best way to go through life--especially when you're only fourteen years old.

Using drugs and alcohol to cope only delays the healing. While you may feel instant relief from your stress and pain, you may completely destroy the possibility of making your life better. You end up keeping your negative thoughts and emotions within you. You never give your thoughts and emotions opportunities to be released and freed because the process would be too painful, draining, and time consuming. You choose to numb your pain with drugs and alcohol because it's quicker, easier and seems like more fun. When you choose to stay in your comfort zone with ineffective coping mechanisms, you may find a short-term fix but not a life-time solution. No matter how difficult a situation may be, you must choose to make life-time fixes if you want a better life.

THE FEAR SEED

Our fears will either motivate us to move ourselves out of our comfort zones and decide to make our life sweeter--or they will keep us trapped. Since fear involves our need to feel safe, we must find enough positive reasoning to move out of our comfort zones before we are willing to take action. We must realize that we will be safe and okay. We can't just say to ourselves, "Okay self, it's time for me to move out of my comfort zone." We have to believe in the reward and repeat the "can-do, will-do" positive thinking affirmations. Instead of saying "I can't," you must begin believing and saying "I can-do, will-do." You can say and do this because you want to, and you deserve to live a more happy and fulfilling life.

Instead of saying "I can't," you must begin believing and saying "I can-do, will-do."

Taking a risk does not mean only negative outcomes can occur. There are also positive outcomes on the other side of a risk. Our negative thinking and worrying can cause stress that can incapacitate us and prevent us from getting what we want in life. They can cause us to go through life feeling so cautious and afraid of doing something wrong or getting hurt that we tread lightly. Many people blame someone else for feeling like they are walking on eggshells. At times, someone else may have acted in a way that caused us anxiety. But many times we place this undue stress on ourselves because of our own insecurities, which have nothing to do with other people. Our self-induced stress can take away our happiness.

When you overcome your fears and begin taking risks, you feel happier, get more done, and stay more involved with life. Instead of acting cowardly, complacent, indecisive and critical of yourself and others, you must realize that something worthwhile and positive is possible on the other side of the risk. Your mindset needs to shift from saying "no" to opportunities because you are fearful, to saying "yes" because you need, want, and deserve a better life.

When in doubt, "always point your tips out." That's what I used to say to myself when I stood safely atop the 11,000 foot massive ski slopes of Colorado. It was my version of, "On your mark, get set, go!" as the tips of my skis pointed out and downhill. Sometimes, my overwhelming fear would freeze me in my stance, at least emotionally. It was easier to stand on top of the mountain and do something else, like take in the majestic mountain scenery, than to let go and face my fear of getting hurt and having a yard sale all over the mountain side. (A yard sale is ski lingo that means wipeout. Imagine skis, ski poles, hats, goggles, etc. sprawled out on a mountain side.)

There were many, many times when I would try to stand extra tall in my five foot, three and three-quarter inch body and muster the courage to give myself that little push that would send me swishing and cruising down the mountainside.

I definitely felt much safer at the top of the mountain with my feet firmly planted on the snow. I always felt like I was in my comfort zone standing still in my skis. Being so high in the sky, I felt like I was safe and protected the way people are when they are in heaven--but I knew that it was not my time to be in heaven. It was my time to be happy, to be free, and just to have a blast! Seeing the slopes full of skiers who were swooshing and soaring down the slopes, showed me that skiing was a doable sport for many--at least for those who find their courage. Whenever I was in doubt and afraid to take on that mountain, I'd point my ski tips out, face my fears and literally say to myself, "You can do it. Hippy, hippy shake." Hippy, hippy shake was to remind me that I needed to use my hips to ski effectively, not to remind me that I have seen the Grateful Dead ninety-six times! I have probably stood on top of a ski slope hundreds, maybe over a thousand times, holding varying degrees of fear within me, but finding my own way down the mountain was my own kind of heaven.

While I did have some pretty wild wipeouts, I never gave up by taking the easy way down on a chairlift. After each

> **When you know that more positive results have occurred than negative results, chances are that your own negative thinking is causing self-induced fears, which will keep you from experiencing many of life's great thrills.**

wipeout, I got back up, wiped the snow off and cruised with extra vigor down the slopes. The feelings of invigoration and accomplishment were tremendous. I felt the thrill of victory. I had to just do it. Each time I skied, I became better at it, and in turn, I increased my confidence, ability, and enthusiasm. Finally, skiing appeared safer and more enjoyable after I had had many positive experiences on the slopes. The only way to understand something fully is to experience it. I wanted to learn how to ski, I was motivated, I was thirsty to make my life sweeter--and I did.

How you choose to respond to your fears will determine whether you make lemonade or stay fearful and sour. It is normal and very okay to feel fearful at times. You need fear to keep you safe from harm's way, but when your fears keep you from living and loving a full life, you need to explore and remove your fear seeds. Whenever you encounter a situation where you feel fearful, you need to realize how many times others overcame their fears and achieved positive results, versus dwelling on those who did not have a favorable outcome. When you know that more positive results have occurred than negative results, chances are that your own negative thinking is causing self-induced fears, which will keep you from experiencing many of life's great thrills.

THE GUILT SEED

Like fear, guilt can keep us from living a happy and fulfilling life. We can feel bad about being happy for doing what we really want to do and asking for what we really need because deep down, we don't think we "should." We believe that we *should* be "people pleasers," putting others first, not ourselves. People who tend to have frequent feelings of guilt also tend to have perfectionist tendencies. They want their environments and the perceptions others hold of them to be perfect, which makes them fearful of making a mistake. They have a much greater inability to let go of grudges since they struggle with admitting that they made any mistakes. Those who have decided not to remove their guilt seeds automatically tend to think they said or did something wrong when conflicts and tough circumstances arise. They believe they are to blame when things go wrong, which makes them think and feel badly about themselves. They can even beat themselves up when they hear about, read about or see others being happy for making their lives better--because they feel inadequate for not doing the same for themselves. They become critical of others, but mostly they become critical of themselves instead of *choosing* to adopt healthy ways of responding to their feelings of guilt.

You gain self-respect and the respect of others when you admit you made a mistake. Respect is a much greater reward than criticism or blame. Instead of being so hard on yourself

> You gain self-respect and the respect of others when you admit you made a mistake.

and others, do something positive to learn from and resolve the situation. It's never too late to realize that you did the best you could with the circumstances you encountered. It's never too late to realize that you are a good person. It's never too late to get happy.

If you have frequent bouts of feeling guilty, you can choose to find peace through forgiveness and appreciation. When you have decided to forgive those who did you wrong--even yourself--and to thank those who did you right, you can find inner peace and gratitude. Forgiveness does not mean that you have to become close friends, or even acquaintances, with those who wronged you, or those you wronged. It just means that you will change your negative thoughts about the person or situation into something positive. This could be as simple as, "Thank goodness that is over and in the past." You end up removing the negativity, which makes room for positive thoughts and peace. Your negativity no longer consumes and controls you. It remains in your past. It's gone, and it's over. You discover this through the compassion and understanding of others and yourself. If you think deeply enough, chances are that even the person who wronged you probably also brought you the gifts of newfound experiences, interests, strength and wisdom. When you are able to tap into your inner wisdom, you can begin to discover the positive lessons learned. If you become open-minded and loving, you will see the good in people and appreciate the experience that was brought into your life. When you remove your guilt seed, you will gain forgiveness and appreciation for yourself and others.

Guilt that brings you a healthy remorse from your circumstances can bring about positive actions. You can begin taking responsibility for your actions and the mistakes you have made by not repeating them in the future. When you own the mistakes you feel guilty about, you can become a better person by doing the right thing next time. Again, this type of healthy remorse requires forgiveness of yourself for the mistakes you have made so you can let go of the past and live for the present and future.

I felt guilt for many reasons for many years. I felt bad that my mother had to work and struggle so much and could not get the love she really deserved. I felt bad that I gave her such a hard, hard time for a few years. I felt bad that my grandmother lived a lonely existence with pain and suffering when we finally had to place her in a nursing home. I felt even worse that my innocent brother had a life of such heartaches and disadvantages, and guilty for leaving him at home alone while I moved around the country.

Even with all my years of heartache and guilt, I learned how to live my life without regrets. If I died today, that would be okay because I found happiness by finally making wise choices. That's not to say that I wouldn't be disappointed and upset about the situation because there still is so much more sweet lemonade out there for me to taste. It's just that at least I know that I gave it my best by saying and doing as much as I could for the ones I love and for myself. When your time or the time of a loved one comes to die, will you have said and done everything you needed to say and do? Instead of revisiting the heartache and guilt I turned into peace in my own life, let me encourage you to live your life without guilt and regrets so you can fully embrace and enjoy all of its goodness.

> When your time or the time of a loved one comes to die, will you have said and done everything you needed to say and do?

THE SHAME SEED

Of all the seeds to discard, shame can have the greatest effect on our self-worth and can be one of the hardest to overcome. It makes us believe that we do not deserve to be happy and treated with respect. We believe this way because we believe we are damaged and flawed. Our feelings of shame are compounded when we think others may discover the truth about our damaged goods. We can try to hide our true selves by maintaining superficial, fake relationships as we build the walls between ourselves and our public identities. When we feel inadequate, we can act phony to feel adequate.

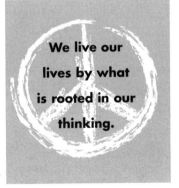

We live our lives by what is rooted in our thinking.

Sometimes we think no one will want us if we are flawed, so we don't expose our authentic selves, in fear of rejection. We might think something is not good about ourselves, so we end up thinking we are not good enough to have our deep, ultimate desires for happiness and peace fulfilled. Like all human beings, we need to be loved and accepted. Like guilt, shame can evolve us into perfectionists and people pleasers. We can end up doing things and getting involved with people who do not treat us the way we deserve. We live our lives by what is rooted in our thinking. If we are ashamed and don't think we deserve very much, then we don't seek life's goodness.

Removing shame seeds is a very slow process. I know because I had more shame seeds than any other seeds. Now, I finally understand that I deserve to be treated with respect, set boundaries, and ask for what I need. The best thing about no longer having shame is that I don't care about how people judge me about the things I did in my past life. I am now proud of myself--not ashamed of myself. I am who I am now and when I screw up, I don't fall back into beating myself up as hard as I once did. Occasionally, when I go to push myself into new, higher heights, it's hard for me to realize that my undeserving self then and my deserving self now are the same person.

When you are a perfectionist and a people pleaser, you are trying to appear wonderful in the eyes of others. You can feel shame when you are not perfect and not putting others first. Perfectionism and people pleasing are stressful and time-consuming and can cause self-induced pressure. No one is perfect and no one can please everyone. When you begin to realize that you are wonderful even with your flaws, you will begin to reduce your stress and self-induced pressure. You will begin letting go of your perfectionist and people-pleasing tendencies. You will begin to realize that you're pretty darn good just the way you are and that you do enough for others.

You will begin pleasing yourself more because you realize that you deserve more. You will utilize your power of choice. You will make peace, love and lemonade.

From what I've been told and the photos I have seen of my childhood, I was a cute, sweet little girl who loved to sing. This is not to be confused with knowing how to sing. I seemed to have been happy being the center of attention, singing to my heart's content. I must have been fearless and secure within myself to sing out loud in front of people. When it came time for my nursery school's play, someone decided to have me sing a solo. I was so excited that I kept singing everywhere I went.

The day of my debut came, and I strolled onto the stage, appearing to be the same happy, brave little girl. Yet on the inside, I was feeling terribly frightened. As I stood at the center of the large stage, it seemed like I was standing on the moon. I stood there quietly in awe as I looked straight ahead and saw all the people in the audience. Their eyes were upon me, ready to pass judgment on my upcoming performance.

I became overwhelmed with fear and stood frozen on the stage, all alone in a much different way than I had been in my play corner at home. It was like the world had stopped. I was numbed by fear and no words would come out of my mouth. I was looking bad in the eyes of others, is what I surely thought. This once-happy, brave girl became sad and afraid.

My compassionate, six-year-old, intellectually-disabled older brother sensed my struggle and brought his unconditional love to the rescue. He walked out onto the stage towards me with a protective pride. He kindly put his arm around my little four-year-old-body and said sweetly, "Let's sing it together, Sis." My mom and, I'm sure, the entire audience, wept with joy. Jeff was always the stronger, more courageous sibling. Even though we sang the song and all the parents wept with joy, to me I had failed. I would carry the shame within me for many, many years. I stopped singing out loud; I stopped doing something I had once really enjoyed.

I feel certain that my embarrassing stage fright was one of the first situations that made me decide to bury my outgoing personality into that of an introvert. For many years, I was insecure and did not want to risk the embarrassing moment ever happening again because I thought nobody would want me if I made mistakes. Heaven forbid if I wasn't perfect in the eyes of others. I decided to take the safe route and not even try to sing anywhere when other people were around. A lemon occurred for me when I failed on stage. Fear and shame were the seeds in my lemon this time.

Holding on to your lemon's seeds of anger, fear, guilt and shame will keep you from making your life better and more gratifying. When you choose to stuff your feelings down and not deal with your emotions, you can experience personal resentment, inner turmoil and emotional numbness. Your choice not to deal with your negative thoughts and emotions, can leave you going through life missing the deep, wonderful happiness and passion that self-expression can bring. Your choice not to bring out your authentic self can leave you going through life dishonestly and superficially. You need to find your courage and deal with your negative thoughts and emotions to live a passionate and fulfilling life. You have a choice.

THE LIGHTHEARTED ZEST

Are you able to lighten up, smile, laugh, act playful, and have fun? Or, do you remain too serious and controlled much of the time? Which would you prefer? You have a choice. You can make a wise choice to grate off your lighthearted zest if you want to live a "zestful" life. Each lemon possesses a powerful, lighthearted zest to help you get through tough times. It needs to be grated off our lemons to help us lighten up during stressful circumstances. Everyone has the ability to smile, laugh, act playful, and have fun. Our abilities just need to be rediscovered if we've been carrying ourselves too seriously for a long time.

When you can bring about laughter and lighten up the tensions of difficult situations, you find some temporary relief. Your smile can brighten up your face and the people around you. Your laugh can energize yourself and the people around you. If you go through life without laughter and lightheartedness, your seriousness and controlled demeanor may evolve into doom, gloom and boredom.

During times of tragedy we just don't have the strength or desire to grate off our lighthearted zest. That's understandable, appropriate and okay. At some point though, we do need some relief from our extremely difficult situations. Remember that every lemon has some zest waiting for us when we need it.

One of the greatest advantages of laughter is that it is free, safe and natural. Sadly, laughter can be uncomfortable for some people who can only be critical of themselves, others and the world around them. They prefer an environment that is orderly and controlled. Laughter and playfulness bring them discomfort because they do not want to let go of their inhibitions and control, or move out of their comfort zones. They may not have experienced much lightheartedness throughout their lives, which makes them uncomfortable in situations with emotional expressiveness and excitement. They can have such fear, of not being seen as perfect in the eyes of others, that they must take themselves seriously and remain in rigid control of their behaviors to feel safe and anxiety-free. They think to themselves, "Oh my goodness, what will people think of me if I let out a large belly laugh or make a goofy face that causes a disruption to the calm?" Or, "Oh my goodness, what will people think of me if I shake my bootie, wave my arms and bob my head when I groove on the dance floor?" Because of their insecurities, these people are missing out on the greatest fun that laughing, dancing and loosening up can bring. Life is hard for everyone some of the time. Chill out, live a little and have some fun!

The medical profession has discovered many healthful benefits of laughter. The ability to laugh at circumstances and ourselves not only releases our body's endorphins, which reduces our stress levels, it brings about smiles that reduce

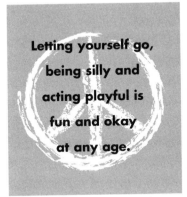

Letting yourself go, being silly and acting playful is fun and okay at any age.

frown lines as we age. Bring some fun and zest into your life once in a while. It's refreshing! Letting yourself go, being silly and acting playful is fun and okay at any age.

"Paaaarrrrty!" is what my brother and I used to say together in our silly, animated way of clenching our fists while raising our arms in the air. Whether it was for a birthday, a Pittsburgh Steelers football game or just raiding the house while our mother was away, my brother and I were the king and queen of celebrating!

Everything we learned about celebrating, hoopla and lightheartedness, we learned from our mother. Even with all of our tough circumstances, Jeff and I were very fortunate to have our fun mother as a positive role model. She loved celebrating large milestones and mini successes. When we had graduations and significant birthdays, we celebrated. When we had successes, she certainly made a fuss in recognition of our achievements. Since the special education field is great at giving people with disabilities ribbons and certificates for many different types of accomplishments, we were a house of celebrations. Jeff's twenty-first birthday was a family favorite.

The house was full of people--many with intellectual disabilities. Plus, Jeff was legally allowed to drink alcohol. He wanted to be like everyone else--he wanted to be accepted and cool. Jeff had a beer. He felt the effects and the entire gang became silly. Everyone strutted onto the street and begin skipping and singing to the "Bunny Hop Trio." We had a blast! In my family, we knew how good it felt to be recognized for our achievements, no matter how large or small. When you celebrate and feel pride in yourself, you feel great!

In addition to celebrating your successes and occasionally lightening up tough times, go experience the world of fun opportunities. You don't need to do anything wild and crazy to have a good time. You just have to get out of the house and experience new people and places that are outside your neighborhood and close circle of friends. Since I am a lover of the live music scene, I can pretty much guarantee that most towns have fairs, festivals and music nearby. They may even be free. Go search for them. Go listen to the music.

This would not be a true peace, love and lemonade book if I did not briefly share my live music experiences. Many people collect items like coins, postage stamps, baseball and YU-GI-OH cards, colored wristbands, Santa Clauses, celebrity memorabilia, etc. I collect concert ticket stubs. Since the 1976 Aerosmith rock show in Pittsburgh's Civic Arena, I have saved the ticket stub from every concert I've attended. I have hundreds. I still love the concert scene. A concert is a time to forget about life for a while, a time to let yourself go away into the music. It's just like Dobie Gray sang, "Oh, give me the beat, boys, and free my soul. I wanna get lost in your rock and roll and drift away." There are no life interferences between all of us and the music. There is a common bond among the crowd. We belong together for those few magical hours. Everyone needs a sense of belonging. When you choose to make peace, love and lemonade, you eventually find where you belong. You are secure, happy, proud, and having fun.

Removing My Lemon Seeds and Grating its Lighthearted Zest Worksheet

From the lemon you selected in Chapter 2, determine what your seeds are. You may have only one kind of seed in your lemon, or you may have all four: anger, fear, guilt and shame. If you first read the question and come up empty with "I don't know," or "I don't have any of these seeds," take some more time to remember your experiences. If your lemon is still bringing you difficulties, chances are your seeds have not been removed. When you choose to make lemonade, find your seeds, remove them and grate off your lighthearted zest.

peace love and lemonade

CHAPTER 3:
REMOVING MY LEMON SEEDS AND GRATING ITS LIGHTHEARTED ZEST WORKSHEET

What Seeds are in My Lemon?	My Responses
What am I angry about with regard to my lemon? Why? How can I forgive myself and others, and appreciate the lemon?	
What do I feel guilty about with regard to my lemon? How can I forgive myself and others, and appreciate the lemon?	
What am I ashamed of with regard to my lemon? Why? How can I forgive myself and others, and appreciate the lemon?	
What can I start feeling lighthearted about with regard to my lemon? Why? How can I learn to appreciate lightheartedness?	
In general what can I do to become more lighthearted in my life?	

> ## CHAPTER 3:
> ## SELF REFLECTION QUESTIONS

The following questions reflect the messages in this chapter. Answer them honestly and decide whether you want to make yourself happier and your life more fulfilling. If your answers to the following questions are mostly "yes" or "often," it's time to consider making some positive changes in your life. Remember, you have the power to make choices for yourself. You have the power to live a great life. You can choose to make lemonade.

Do I consistently think negative thoughts and hold negative emotions?

Do I have a difficult time knowing what I feel or how to express my feelings?

Do I have a difficult time being lighthearted, celebrating successes or having fun?

Do I have a difficult time forgiving myself and others for past mistakes?

Do I have a difficult time appreciating the people and experiences I have encountered?

CHAPTER 4:
STIR UP YOUR GREATNESS POTENTIAL SWEETENERS

Greatness Potential Sweeteners

COURAGE

ASSERTIVENESS

PASSION

Would you prefer to stay stuck or live a happy life? Living a happier life makes me want to jump into the middle of Grant Street in downtown Pittsburgh. As I leap into the air, I toss my hat into the air and begin singing out loud the lyrics to the old Mary Tyler Moore television show theme song: "You're gonna make it after all!" After I release my exhilarating excitement, I feel a deep sense of pride because I have found my greatness potential.

Your greatness potential is like the sugar that has settled at the bottom of your refreshingly sweet glass of lemonade. It's inside the glass; it's inside you. It's there for you when you can't take life anymore. It's there for you when you're willing to make a change.   Like the sugar at the bottom of the glass, it can become stuck. Stir it up! It's holding in your courage, assertiveness and passion, which are necessary sweeteners to make lemonade. You need to stir them up once in a while to taste the sweetness of life. You need to act with courage, to communicate with assertiveness and to find your passion if you want to make your life sweeter. Just like the taste of lemonade, imagine how weak, sour and bitter your life will be without any sugar. Lemonade needs sugar just like you need courage, assertiveness and passion to reach your greatness potential.

Since the day you were born, your environment and experiences have shaped you into who you are today. Every single person you met, every single object you saw, every single smell you smelled and every single sound and word you heard made you think and behave the way you do to this very day. If you had experiences in your life that empowered you to use your courage, you probably think and act in courageous ways. If you had experiences in your life that stifled your courage, you might not think and act in courageous ways. In other words, if you were told over and over again that you can't do something, and if you did not receive the nurturing and love necessary to feel good about yourself, you might think that you're not capable and deserving of being happy. You may say to yourself, "That's just for other people. Why should I even try?"

After hearing, you "can't" do something often, you begin believing you "can't" and accept the status quo. Challenging the status quo and being courageous shakes things up and goes against the norm, which many conforming types do not like. Some of your friends may no longer want to be your friends. Others may criticize you, and what you are becoming involved with because *they* may be feeling rejected, inadequate or envious. They may not support you while you go through the "changing curve."

To maintain your focus, ask yourself, "Is my role to make everyone else happy, or myself?" To make your life happier, your answer will have to be "to make myself happy." To make yourself happy, you need courage, assertiveness and passion. Find them.

Stir up your greatness that has been suppressed. Sometimes in life, we end up settling for whatever comes our way. We just go with the way things are instead of pursuing what could be better for us. We lose our courage, assertiveness and passion.

To be certain that your life stays fresh and fulfilling, keep stirring up your courage, assertiveness and passion sweeteners. When you are ready to make another change, you can stir them up again and again to find your greatness potential. Bring your greatness back into your life and enjoy your lemonade.

COURAGE

For his entire forty-six years, my brother, Jeff, was a man of great courage. No matter what the circumstance, he put forth effort and gave his best. He didn't care as much about winning as simply being a player in the game. I know he felt disappointment when he did not win because he would either frown, shrug his shoulders or say, "Rats." He accepted his limitations and failures, yet he continued to try and get involved. Involvement was good enough for him. Jeff loved life. He wanted to be a part of any activity and family gathering he could. We always got him charged up about how he had a better social life than our mother and me combined. Besides our outings and travels together, he went out and about on many organized trips for people with disabilities, even all the way to Hawaii. He was so excited when I made a big fuss over him going *all* the way to Hawaii while I was stuck working in Pittsburgh. Boy, did he think he was cool. I loved when I could get him to smile and show excitement the way he did. His happy-guy trademark was taking both his fists up to his cheeks, then rubbing and rolling them around while smiling the entire time. I loved that joyous expression. I loved him.

Unfortunately, my brother unexpectedly became seriously ill with end-stage renal disease complications. On a clear summer day, around 11:00 a.m. on a Friday, and seven weeks after his forty-sixth birthday celebration, I received a call from

Jeff's group-home caregiver. She said, "Jeff passed out and we are in the emergency room."

When I arrived, Jeff was conscious and looking at me with oxygen tubes in his nose. I gave my usual greeting, "Hey Bro, what's going on?"

He gave me his usual shoulder shrug meaning, "I don't know." He just looked at me.

His beautiful, golden-green eyes touched my soul once again. To this day, I cannot recall any words he said. But I do recall his caregiver telling me that, right before I walked into the room, Jeff had said, "Where's my sister? She should be here by now." My memory recalls these as the last words he ever spoke.

Little did I realize then that my favorite guy was dying. Within minutes, Jeff's health went downhill until he could no longer breathe on his own and needed an emergency intubation because his oxygen level had dropped significantly. He was placed on a ventilator to keep him alive. Then within another few minutes, his only kidney stopped functioning. One afternoon, about two weeks into his traumatic time, I was sitting by his bedside. I had tears in my eyes when he woke. A small tear rolled out of his right eye. I asked, "Bro, are you scared?" He gave a weak nod. I said, "Me too." After Jeff received a tracheotomy, we were struggling to get him to speak.

It was difficult to know if he didn't want to cooperate or simply couldn't speak due to the trauma he had received. It was time to push him harder. I said, "Bro, you have to try to talk." He looked at me and did not try. In a much firmer voice I asked, "Bro, do you want to live?" He struggled and crookedly mouthed "yes." Jeff tried. He found his courage. Jeff remained in the ICU for five weeks of small triumphs, but much pain and suffering.

The time finally came when we decided to give Jeff peace. This man of great courage was also a man of great will; Jeff wasn't quitting this fight for life. He fought and tried to be with us for five days without life support. I'm sure he struggled between wanting relief from his suffering and wanting to stay with us. The greatest act of courage that I have ever seen came the night before we were to start his terminal weaning off the ventilator. My brother showed me how to be brave, how to be strong when we know we're about to face one of life's most scary times: death.

Even with his intellectual disabilities and deteriorating health, he was aware, strong and brave. He lay still in the night, his eyes glistening with a calm serenity. He knew he would soon be leaving us. He knew that he had to be brave and let things happen as they were going to happen. He was calm with peace. I was calm with fear.

Courage is the power behind all the steps and ingredients that make lemonade.

In my overwhelming state of wanting to have everything be one thousand percent perfect for my brother, I still struggle when I think that I could have sat up from my sleeping chair to reach out and comfort him instead of just sitting next to him as I did. It was one of his final conscious moments over the next five days, and I believe I "should" have been more aware of that timing. I couldn't overcome my own fear at that moment.

A friend told me that Jeff was showing me how to die. I guess she was right, because I have never seen such a brave man or woman. Let us all be so brave and courageous when our time comes. Let us make our lives sweeter before our time comes to leave our loved ones.

My brother's death was definitely a very difficult time for me. It's been a long healing process that has required me to make lemonade. While my heavy, heavy grief has lifted, I still need my brother's courage and always will. My brother's courage will help me find peace with the loss of him and our lifestyle. It will help me instill a bigger love within me from all the unconditional love he gave me. Finally, it will help me create lemonade for my future.

Courage is the power behind all the steps and ingredients that make lemonade. It is the power behind choice. It takes courage to determine your lemons and their seeds. It takes courage to grate off your lightheaded zest once in a while. It takes courage to act assertively and find your passion. Finally, it takes courage to become accountable for your actions, think positively and believe in yourself. It takes courage to choose to make lemonade.

Whenever you face problems in life and work, there will always be an element of fear. When you demonstrate courage, you are taking action to face and overcome your fears. Acting on your fears is the hardest thing to do because fear is driven from your core being. Finding courage is the most important action step for a happier life. When you honestly want something, you will find your courage and take action. Want good things to happen for you. Make wise choices for yourself regardless of your fears and obstacles.

The choices we make are a direct reflection of the courage we find to take a chance. Napoleon Hill once said, "The person who complains that he or she never had a chance probably hasn't the courage to take a chance." Everyone has fears. Everyone has obstacles. Everyone has lemons with seeds but only the brave make peace, love and lemonade because they know the reward is sweeter than the struggle they may have endured.

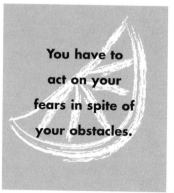

You have to act on your fears in spite of your obstacles.

With any challenge, there is a chance of mistakes and failure. On the flipside of challenge, there is a chance of achievement and success. Fear of failure consumes us and can make us stay stuck. We choose not to try, and become complacent. When we learn from our mistakes and failures what won't work and what to avoid the next time, we become smarter. This new knowledge increases our chances of success.

Your risk-taking equals your desire to find courage. You need courage even for taking calculated risks. To take a risk means finding courage to move beyond your familiar comfort zone. Whether you change your hairstyle, return a cold meal or decide to live a better life, you have to act on your fears in spite of your obstacles. This is courage. You cannot change, grow or progress without it. You may have fewer opportunities to fail by not taking risks, but the negative energy from being stuck, unhappy and complacent surely outweighs the feelings of happiness. Find the courage and feel the "can-do, will-do" exhilarating attitude.

The first step to finding courage is to realize your fears. When you have completed the fear seed worksheet and the attitude worksheet in the next section, see what is holding you back from taking action--from finding your courage. Your obstacles are your fears. Quite often your fears are exaggerated and very personal. When you dig deep and discover your true needs and desires, you will find courage to act on your fears.

Tears represent truth. When you feel either happy or sad, with tears coming into your eyes, look for your truths. The next time you cry, ask yourself, "What truth about me are my tears telling me? What do my tears mean for me?" Forget about everyone and everything else. Simply focus on yourself. Everyone deserves a moment of "me-time." To get the best discoveries from your "me-times," spend time alone without anyone or anything to distract you from your reflective thinking. Many people are afraid to spend time alone; however, listening to your best friend, yourself, is a great way to discover your truths and needs.

Find the courage to talk with someone who can be objective and supportive with you. You are better off not being around people who bring you down with negative, draining energy, and those who usually respond to you with reactions like, "You're crazy! You'll never do it! It can't be done!" They are dealing with their own fears and negative thoughts. They will make you second-guess your efforts. Don't let them!

You have to persevere regardless of what others may think or say about you. You cannot let others' false assumptions and insecure judgments stop you from supporting your core beliefs and pursuing your dreams. Realize that as you grow and move forward with your life, some of your friends and acquaintances will feel threatened and respond in unfavorable ways by dismissing you with words like, "Oh, you're too good for us now."

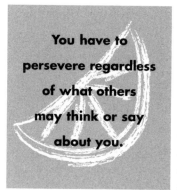

You have to persevere regardless of what others may think or say about you.

It's not that you became too good for others. You have just found courage to explore new horizons that are bringing you new interests. You have discovered new ways of living that make you happy. You may have outgrown each other and perhaps, the relationship was not as genuine as you once thought. It is a reality that people will not connect with or be liked by everyone they meet. You can continue to maintain long-time friends and make new ones.

Some friendships tend to cycle. We may or may not continue spending time with the same friends as we move through life. We may even recognize at a later time that someone important was in our life all along. We just didn't get to know them because of our own insecurities and false judgments. Eventually when we are open-minded and ready, we make friends with people who are best for us.

If you spend energy trying to please and seek approval by everyone, you will be wasting energy that could be used to bring you success and happiness. The more diverse experiences and friends you have, the richer and healthier your life is. Find and learn from someone who demonstrates the traits you desire to cultivate within yourself. It takes courage to find people who already have obtained the traits you desire. This realization makes you acknowledge that you are not perfect and that you have room for improvement. That's okay. We all have room for improvement.

Since people tend to hang around those who are similar to themselves, your traits will begin to evolve like theirs. Having people around you who provide support and mentorship, will help you build your confidence and "can-do, will-do" attitude. When we surround ourselves with people who bring out the best within us, our experiences are richer.

Ask yourself and the person who possesses the traits you would like to have, "What am I more afraid of, failure or success?" You will be amazed by what you discover. Sometimes, you end up creating what you fear most; without even being consciously aware, your thinking is influencing your daily decision making. With each decision you make, you affect your future. If you tend to be wishy-washy and delay your decision making, you cannot expect much to be different in a timely manner. The only way to know if a certain result will occur is actually to try, as my brother always did.

ASSERTIVENESS

In America, we are allowed to work in careers we choose that bring us fulfillment, passion and wealth. We have the freedom and opportunities to live the lives we want. We are allowed to have and express our own opinions and feelings. We can appropriately and respectfully ask that our needs get met. It's okay to assert ourselves. It's okay to say "no." So many others do, why not you, too?

Everyone deserves to be happy. To become truly happy you need to adopt an assertive behavior approach. Decide whether you will meet the expectations of others or head in directions that are unique to you without disrespecting other people. If you are searching for deeper relationships, a loving home, or advancement in your career, you need to begin respectfully sharing your honest thoughts, needs and feelings, without regard for another's approval, or fear of disapproval or rejection.

When a co-worker or even your boss, gives you another "to-do-today" action item, do you consistently say "yes" when you want to say "no" because your workload is already extremely overloaded? Or do you say, "I want to help you. What's your timeline? Here's what's on my plate now. Let's figure out some options to fulfill your request."

In your personal life, what happens if your hairstylist gives you a bad do? Do you go home and cry in front of the mirror and wear a hat until your hair grows back? Or do you say something like, "I'm feeling uncomfortable with this style and prefer my bangs to be longer. Please take less off the next time."

Another common scenario you may have experienced is when the dinner you're *paying for* is served cold. Do you withdraw into silence and eat cold food? Or do you attack with dominance, become critical and demand that your food come back hot? Or do you simply say, "My food is cold. I need to have it heated."

When you react with respect for yourself and others, respect and a sweeter life will come your way. Of course, you must use your best judgment in deciding which battles to address and which to let go. Depending on the situation you are facing, you can approach your situations with aggressive, passive or assertive reactions. Many assume that the way they behave is just the way they are by saying things like, "This is just who I am," or, "That's just the way he or she is." In truth, it is not how you are; it's how you are choosing to be. When you *choose* to be aggressive, you are saying, "It's all about me baby. I don't respect you. I'm in control here."

When you *choose* to be passive, you are saying, "It's all about you Mr. or Ms. Superior. I don't respect me. I don't want any conflicts that could cause a stressful situation and rejection." As Eleanor Roosevelt said, "No one can make you feel inferior without your consent." You deserve respect.

When you *choose* to be assertive you are saying, "It's all good. I respect you, and I respect me. Let's try to understand and resolve this together." The assertive approach is appropriate for most situations. It brings win-win results. It brings about the confidence and respect necessary to pursue your aspirations both professionally and personally. Whether you are stating your expectations at work or home, you will receive more positive results with assertive behaviors.

> When you *choose* to be assertive you are saying, "It's all good. I respect you, and I respect me. Let's try to understand and resolve this together."

There are no perfect solutions to life's pressures, because there are no perfect people. While it is usually best to strive for assertiveness, there are times when both aggressive and passive behaviors are appropriate. For example, in a critical emergency situation, fast and even abrupt decisions must be made, which can require aggressive behaviors. When emotions are highly fueled, it's best to become passive until the situation calms. A time when a more passive approach is warranted is when we assume a new leadership position. It is best to begin the role by observing and seeking input from others before making changes. This will help reduce resistance and increase buy-in to change.

As you adopt the assertive approach, conflicts will arise with the people you encounter along the way. When you find the courage to be assertive, you are telling people how their ways of being are affecting and hurting you. By sharing your expectations and feelings, you are reducing frustrations, mistakes and false assumptions. This, in turn, earns you respect from others and earns you respect within yourself, too.

THE DIFFERENCES BETWEEN AGGRESSIVE, PASSIVE AND ASSERTIVE BEHAVIOR

AGGRESSIVE

	AGGRESSIVE
Behavior Traits	Disrespectfully direct and honest, bossy, closed off, reactive; acts from fears of not being right and in control
Purpose	To win, dominate and control
What are the general perceptions of someone who demonstrates the behavior?	An angry, controlling, perhaps spiteful, mean-spirited person with low self-esteem
How does the sender feel about him or herself during and after the interaction?	Superior, relieved, in control, perhaps aftermath guilt for behaving disrespectfully
Self-development question	Why am I so afraid and insecure about not being in control and not being right that I end up hurting and pushing everyone away?

*To evaluate and understand your own behaviors,
the following chart can guide your future actions.*

PASSIVE	ASSERTIVE
Indirect and dishonest, minimal self-disclosure, reactive; retreats into silence, acts from fears of conflict and rejection	Respectfully direct and honest, self-disclosing and open-minded, collaborative, proactive; acts from courage and choice
To avoid conflict, and please people	To achieve a win-win situation and openness
A person who doesn't speak up and will let people walk all over him or her, can't trust his or her word, a "doormat" with low self-esteem	A trusting, caring respected person with healthy self-esteem
Anxious, inferior, incompetent, taken for granted, compromising, controlled, disrespected	Confident, self-respecting, empathic now and later for behaving respectfully
Why am I so afraid of rejection that I can't ask for what I honestly want and need?	Do I feel good for being true to myself and compassionate for others?

Passive and aggressive people tend to hold irrational beliefs. They think life's challenges will go away if they avoid dealing with them or if they blast someone. They think they can get an immediate quick fix. This is short-term thinking, and long-term thinking usually is necessary if we want to improve our work and personal performances and relationships. In some cases, the problem may go away immediately, but people who take these approaches still tend to end up frustrated and unfulfilled because they consistently decide to deal with their problems with short-term fixes.

At the beginning of this book, I said it is not going to be easy to make peace, love and lemonade. To think and act for long-term results will require appropriate assertive reactions toward people and situations. Becoming assertive is a long-term process of developing skills, confidence, self-respect and the respect of others. To become more assertive requires a one-attempt-at-a-time approach, due to the fear and anxiety that is involved in making the transformation. It is a hard, ongoing effort that requires a thought-out process before approaching the person(s) involved or situation. To make matters more challenging, there may not be any desirable solutions for a particular situation. When this is the case, then all you can do is be brave just like my brother was while he was fighting for his life. Do the best you can even if it is frightening and difficult. Accept that "it is what it is."

When you begin to understand yourself and your needs, you will know what to communicate assertively as your boundaries, expectations and feelings with others. You will have more free time because you will have fewer conflicts and greater fulfillment from communicating more assertively and tolerating less. Stating your boundaries and expectations gives you more "me-time." Get your "me-time." Expect with each moment of effort and initiative, there will be some successes and failures. This is just the natural part of going through the "changing curve." It's an awkward time. When you learn from your mistakes and failures by doing things differently the next time around, success will come your way. As you begin seeing the positive results from your assertive actions you will start to make your own peace, your own love, and your own lemonade. Imagine how much more energy and time you will have as you take control of your life for the long-term.

I am Assertive! Worksheet

Use the following questions to begin the process of gaining self-respect and the respect of others by becoming assertive. Reflect on the lemon you selected previously. Write your responses to discover how you are about to become assertive. Exercise seven will require you to continuously repeat your new positive affirmation. With practice, "I am assertive and courageous." can become ingrained in your belief system.

CHAPTER 4:
I AM ASSERTIVE! WORKSHEET

Assertiveness Questions	My Assertiveness Applied
What is the situation I want to handle assertively?	
What is my desired outcome of this situation?	
What is keeping me from being assertive?	
What do I need to say, think and do differently?	
What are the consequences if I don't handle this situation assertively?	
What are the rewards if I do handle this situation assertively?	
Each night before I fall asleep and each morning as soon as I wake up, I will say to myself ten times, "I am assertive and courageous."	
Each day, I will take a 15-minute "me-time" break to do what?	

PASSION

Are you saying and doing things because you "should" or because you "want to"? Chances are if you're living a life of "shoulds," you are not living a passionate life that is unique for you. You are living a life by what you believe you are "supposed" to do, according to society and people around you. Living a life of "shoulds" can bring you a life of complacency, frustration, boredom and perhaps dread. When you begin living your life according to your unique interests, talents and values, you will be doing things because you really need and want to for your own happiness and fulfillment. You will really be diggin' life. This does not mean you are to become irresponsible and do as you please without regard to others. It means you need to realize *why* you are doing what you are doing.

Our anxious feelings can help us realize the driving reasons for our actions. Our anxious feelings could represent normal, nervous excitement. Or, they could mean we are embarking on something that is not aligned with our core values and beliefs. If the latter is the case, we are not living with integrity. We are not being our authentic selves.

When you live by doing things you really want for yourself, you will be challenged to do some hard work. It takes great effort to achieve your greatness potential. The effort of changing may require doing things you don't enjoy as much but are necessary to achieve what you really want in life. For example, to have this book published to help people grow, I must make the time to do the cumbersome, sometimes grueling writing and editing to get it done. As they say, "No pain, no gain."

The beginning of the process was what I dreaded most. I kept procrastinating, getting stuck and saying to myself, "Ugh, I don't wanna today. Do I have to? Yes Nancy, you have to (rang the words of my great therapist)." Each time I sat at my computer, I would talk to myself and say, "I want to write this book." I did not say, "I should write this book." My wanting made writing much easier for me, though I will admit, I did have many crazed moments of crunching pretzels and eating Twizzlers. My nervous excitement, anxiety and feelings of being overwhelmed got the best of me at times. Eventually, I would get in the groove and feel my energizing passion for writing my book. My inner drive pushed my fingertips forward to type the words. As I wrote more and more, I saw my confidence build. My dread and anxiety dissipated. Quite often, I actually enjoyed it. As I was nearing the end, I really began diggin' it!

At the beginning of writing this book, I did not know how the final content, layout and design would evolve. I did know my vision and understood that a long process and learning curve were involved. I did know that I would continuously write and rewrite each manuscript draft. I knew I would not have much of book on draft one, two or three. I estimated that it would take about ten. It actually took eleven drafts plus the preliminary writing stage to reach the point it is at today. I realize that even after it has been published, it will have plenty of room for additional improvements.

This is the natural progression of success and achievement. It takes time, effort and practice to reach our dreams. You can procrastinate and put off what you really want because of the time, effort, courage and discipline that is needed. You may imagine your tasks to be larger and harder than they actually are. Your imagination and fears can prevent you from getting started. Once you get started, the tasks get easier, which allows you to get more accomplished. You end up feeling great surges of energy and your confidence builds.   Your energy and confidence fuel you with passion. You start, you learn, you master, you succeed, you dig life--though you still need effort, courage and discipline!

Another risk of pursuing your passions is that others will not possess the same passions. If you expect everyone to get as high as you are when you are passionate about something, you will become disappointed when they are not. For example, of all the people reading my book, some will like it, some will not. That's just the rejection reality that I understand and accept.

If you remain too fearful of rejection, you will miss out on living a happier life. Do what's best for you to make yourself happy and fulfilled. This does not mean you have to become totally self-absorbed and keep pushing your passions and interests onto others. Actually, that pushes people away. Find kindred spirits who share your passions, ideas and activities. Together, you will be exhilarated and energized by the great support and fun you give each other.

Take another "me-moment" and think about why you are working at the job you do and the reasons you are staying friends and lovers with the people in your life. Do the reasons have real meaning to you? Do they support your unique needs and your desire to live a happier life?

Over the years, I have heard many people complain about their jobs, friends and their love lives. While a certain degree of negativity and venting are normal and necessary, you have the opportunity to *choose* whether or not to stay in the same miserable and unhealthy work and personal environments. You can choose whether to stay stuck with your lemons or you can choose to make lemonade. Think about it: are you really happy with your job, the kind of work you do and your personal relationships?

Typical responses for not ending a personal relationship revolve around not wanting to be alone and not wanting to deal with the drama and heartache that can occur when ending a personal relationship. Many others talk about the qualities they hope will change in the other person. There never is a good time to end a relationship. It is the pain of letting go that understandably, we want to avoid. If you know what your values are, you know what you need in your personal relationships. Everyone has unique values. Life is so much easier and happier when we are paired with people who share similar values--not superficial interests. It does not matter if you have different hobbies, as much as if you can appreciate, accept and be open to the person participating in them without you. If one person is open-minded and flexible and the other person is closed-minded and stubborn, rifts will occur. Or, if one person is expressive and the other person is not a communicator, frustrations and miscommunications will mount. You must decide what is important to you in your personal relationships, and you must not settle for less than you deserve.

By giving yourself time to be alone you can make these decisions and keep yourself open and available until that right, unique person for you comes into your life. You just have to find the courage to be alone and go through the process of letting go and moving forward. If you choose to find a deep, passionate happiness, you are choosing to make lemonade.

Typical responses for staying in a job usually revolve around needing a paycheck and the hassles searching for a new job can bring. What people who stay stuck in a dead-end job are really saying to themselves is, "I just don't deserve to be happy. I am not worthy of living a passionate, happy life. I'm settling at this

> **Whatever type of work you choose to do will be much more enjoyable if it expands upon your authentic values.**

job because it's easier."

Whatever type of work you choose to do will be much more enjoyable if it expands upon your authentic values. If the work you do stems from someone telling you that it is what you *should* do or because the money is great, chances are you're working a really long, stressful week. If you choose to stay in a job that does not excite you, at least discover a hobby or special interest that does. When you discover what you really enjoy and are good at, the courage necessary for risk-taking becomes much easier to find. You will have an inner drive that gets you up each morning, ready to embrace each experience with confidence and contagious enthusiasm.

All too often, when people retire and no longer have their professional identification tags and roles, they don't know who they are and how to carry themselves through the later years of life. They may end up feeling bad about themselves and regretful about what they did or did not do. We know that rarely is a negative word spoken about people after they die. But truly and honestly, what do you want people to say about you when you're gone?

Think about who you are and what you are doing with

your life instead of being known for what kind of work you do. At any point in your life, you can discover the true identity that has been covered up behind your work. You have so much more within you that your profession masks. When you make a conscious effort at self-discovery, joy can prevent many of the depressing moments that can occur when you are older.

My mother has this sweet man, Don, in her life now. I recall a friend of his friend saying the most wonderful words about his character at Don's retirement party. He said, "Don is the most kind and compassionate man I have ever known." I remember thinking that really is the highest honor anyone can receive.

When I was twenty, before I stirred up my greatness potential sweeteners, I had to punch in on the time clock for an amusement park job I really wasn't enjoying. My job title was games hostess, a.k.a. "carnie." Each summer day I would walk down the amusement park's causeway, wearing the dorkiest uniform and full of dread. It had two pieces--royal blue culottes and a white shirt with Ferris wheels imprinted all over it. As you can probably assume correctly, way back then I was miserable and rebellious; I definitely was not into wearing skirts!

As with all routines, I eventually became comfortable with my uniform and programmed job tasks of asking people to play my game, taking their money and giving them prizes. I did so in a very monotone, matter-of-fact manner. At this point in my life, I was introverted. I had no passion. I was unhappy.

When I first attempted this job, I was really awful at it. I was boring, with my burned-out, introverted, monotone voice. I do recall my supervisors telling me to put some "oomph" into the microphone. I was getting on-the-job training to improve my skills and keep me from getting fired. The training may have helped me decide to stir up my greatness potential sweeteners.

My hunch is that I was realizing that I was failing once again, and I didn't want to fail anymore. I was *afraid* that I would be fired. I wanted to stay away from home and make it on my own. I needed to do this job well. I was thirsty for lemonade.

One day I chose to stir things up in my dreaded job. My supervisor took notice, and I will never forget what happened that day when I decided to stir up my courage, assertiveness and passion. I talked to myself and said, "Nance, you gotta get this right today. Let yourself go. Do it Nance. Do it Nance." Wow, was I a different person. That day, I decided to make my own peace, my own love, and my own lemonade. Boy, was it sweet!

When I stirred up my greatness potential sweeteners, all of the courage, assertiveness and passion that had been stifled and squelched within me, finally became free. I finally became me. I let down my guard and let go of my insecurities. I began making peace with my past; instilling love within myself from greater confidence; and creating lemonade for my happier, more fulfilling future. I became alive with passion and enthusiasm. I started shouting into the microphone, "TWENTY-FIVE CENTS TO PLAY, TWENTY-FIVE CENTS TO WIN, COME ON IN!" Wow! Who was that?!

I can vividly recall my supervisor coming up to me and saying, "Way to go. What did you do, eat a peanut butter and jelly sandwich?" I guess that was his way of saying, "Good job." That exhilarating, successful moment changed me forever. I found my first real success in my life when I became the best carnie in town. Amazingly, I became successful overnight with my newfound talent.

I truly believe that awesome feeling of being able to achieve something was the "official" starting point of my healing journey. At this point, I finally found a bit of confidence and started having a blast! I came to love that job so much that I went on to be a carnie at the state fair of Texas for a couple of seasons. I was finally opening up, like a singing child. My newfound confidence in my abilities helped me start feeling better.

Success and fun are always how you individually define them. Now a clean-cut professional, I found my first bout of confidence by whooping and hollering into a microphone, "Twenty-five cents to play, twenty-five cents to win, come on in!" For old time's sake, I must share my favorite line, "July is your winner... did you lie to me baby or tell me the truth...

Juh lie." I still say that phrase every July with a sense of pride and a smile. I loved being a carnie with its fast-paced energy, but mostly, I loved that I finally could do something besides drugs and alcohol. Sixteen years after my traumatic stage-fright experience, I finally was finally becoming assertive and overcoming my fear of speaking in front of people. This was the best party I had ever had. I felt the magic of passion.

Passion makes it easier and more worthwhile for you to get out of bed each morning and enjoy your day.

Living a life and working a job that brings you enthusiasm and empowerment gives you passion. You don't necessarily have to jump up in the air with exhilaration all the time. When you are passionate, you will just feel happy about what you are doing with your time. Passion makes it easier and more worthwhile for you to get out of bed each morning and enjoy your day.

I am Passionate! Worksheet

Use the following questions on the next page to begin the process of bringing passion into your life. Reflect throughout your entire life on all the times you felt happy and fulfilled. What were you doing? Differentiate in this worksheet between the activities when you felt simple enjoyment and those when you felt charged and energized. This awareness will help you determine what *could* bring you passion. Your lists will help you decide what you need to bring into your life.

CHAPTER 4:
I AM PASSIONATE! WORKSHEET

Passion Questions	My Passion Applied
What are some things that I have liked doing in the past and currently enjoy doing? 1. 2. 3. 4. 5.	What are some things that I have liked doing in the past and currently absolutely love doing? 1. 2. 3. 4. 5.
What are some things that I really miss doing? 1. 2. 3. 4. 5.	What are some the things that I always wanted to do in my lifetime? 1. 2. 3. 4. 5.
What are some activities that I no longer need in my life? 1. 2. 3.	From the lists above, what acitivty(ies) will I bring into my life? 1. 2. 3.

CHAPTER 4:
SELF REFLECTION QUESTIONS

The following questions reflect the messages in this chapter. Answer them honestly and decide whether you want to make yourself happier and your life more fulfilling. If your answers to the following questions are mostly "yes" or "often," it's time to consider making some positive changes in your life. Remember, you have the power to make choices for yourself. You have the power to live a great life. You can choose to make lemonade.

Do I have trouble saying "no"?

Do I say to myself, "That's just for other people. Why should I even try?"

Do I have people in my life telling me, "You're crazy. You'll never do it! It can't be done!"

Am I afraid of failing or of being successful?

Have I been saying to myself, "This is just who I am"?

Do I consider myself to be consistently (answer separately) aggressive, passive or assertive?

Am I not getting my "me-time"?

Am I saying and doing things mostly because I "should"?

Am I truly not happy with my job or personal relationships?

Do I not know who I authentically am or what I want to be when I "grow up"?

> ## CHAPTER 5:
> ## THE BEST LEMONADE EVER

Being born into a broken, unhappy home forty-six years ago, I discovered early on that the secret mixing method to making life sweeter takes a big pinch of courage. No matter how hard the effort was I had to at least try and give it my best. No matter how tough life was, I realized that I had to do something positive, think something positive and especially believe something positive to make something positive happen.

I learned so much and became rich inside from two amazingly strong-willed people: my mother, Carol, and my brother, Jeff ("Bro"). They were handed so many lemons, probably an entire orchard, if I counted all of them. You know what they did? They made the best lemonade ever, and I learned how to make my life sweeter from them. They were my very small, fun and hectic family.

In the sixties, women did not leave their abusive husbands; furthermore, the Catholic Church kicked out women, like my mother, for finding the courage to protect herself and her children. My mother had married her high school sweetheart and cherished her "Cinderella" dream of living happily ever after with her first love.

After one year of being newlyweds, they were the proud parents of twin boys, Randy and Jeff. Sadly, after six months, Randy died of cardiovascular complications. My mother

It's never too late to be what you could have been.

buried her innocent child. The pain she and my father must have felt was too much for them to bear. Their high school sweetheart marriage fell apart and at the age of twenty-five, my mother found herself sitting on the steps, locked outside of our row house with two toddlers and some of our belongings scattered out on the lawn. She was painfully betrayed and had no place to call home that first very scary night on her own. She had no home, no job, and no money--but she did have two kids, whom she loved. My mother's sweet dream of living happily-ever-after had become her nightmare. Her life was changed forever. Embarrassed and ashamed now, she courageously stood in the welfare line and signed on the line where it stated: I am poor; I have no money; I have two kids and myself to feed, clothe and shelter.

Fortunately, my mother had the determination to do something about her tough, tough circumstance. She found the force, stamina and strength to provide a better life for herself and her children. She quickly chose not to live on welfare. As a single parent, she persevered to earn enough money as a secretary to take herself out of the welfare line. On her own she would pay for life's expenses like rent for the one-bedroom apartment where the three of us slept in the same bed for a few years. There were many nights when my mother slept alone on the couch. While working full-time, she provided for two kids: one intellectually-disabled son and one out-of-control, rebellious daughter. Remarkably, she did so while attending nine years of night school. She earned her bachelor's degree at the University of Pittsburgh and, finally, her law degree at Duquesne University, at the age of thirty-seven. Being born into this inspiring way of surviving taught me that it's never too late to be what you could have been.

When I was eight years old, we moved up and out of our one-bedroom apartment to a better neighborhood. We were fortunate to have my grandmother, Nanny, move into our rented duplex and take care of us for a few solid years until we had to take care of her. Unfortunately, Nanny became senile, as we called it back then. Today, the disorder is known as Alzheimer's disease.

After her memory deteriorated, we would find Kleenex and hard-shelled peanuts scattered in the oddest of places around the house. She also was cold most of the time and developed some rather bizarre patterns of wearing her clothes, like putting on two dresses at the same time with a cardigan sweater or outdoor coat while she was indoors. Nanny also had hallucinations of seeing her late husband, Heinie, up in the kitchen cabinets. In her old, crackling voice, I can recall her pointing her crooked, finger and shouting, "Heinie get down from there!" Our house surely wasn't boring! Yet through all the mayhem and chaos as a single parent, my mother always managed somehow to provide for us.

My mother was on her way to making her own peace, love and lemonade. When she was finally enjoying the rewards of her successes, she was given not one but two more hardships, ten years apart. She survived two separate diagnoses of breast cancer and endured two separate mastectomies. My mother is a survivor, a thriver and a wonderful role model for anyone facing hard times. Now, that's lemonade! You choose: if you were in the same situation as my mother was, would you have decided to stay stuck and complacent on welfare or would you have decided to do something different and more challenging like my mother did?

The second lemonade story involves my brother, whom I called "Bro." He truly always had the biggest part of my heart, happiness and worry. A carefree spirit, Jeff did not harbor negativity from his difficult times. Sure, he felt down at times when life was hard, but his reactions were peaceful, loving and harmonious. His most commonly used word was, "whatever." He didn't "sweat the small stuff" and found something positive in every situation--those good things called silver linings. Jeff was a person who always gave others his unconditional love. The many hurtful experiences he endured gave him and me the greatest gifts that anyone can have. These gifts are the beauty of compassion and kindness for all people, no matter how different they may be. The mean-spirited encounters of teasing and ridicule that made my brother feel unwanted and unloved gave him a big and gentle heart that would never reciprocate the hurt he received.

Jeff was handed his first lemon when his twin brother died. I'm sure he felt the loss that something was different, something was missing. Then, Jeff had his own health issues when he had seizures as an infant. These seizures caused many scary, traumatic times for both my brother and my mother. No one knows what caused the seizures. The seizures did cause my brother to have intellectual disabilities, with an IQ of 73, which is considered mild, borderline mental retardation. His IQ relates to a grown man having the developmental abilities of a twelve-year-old boy. At the onset of adolescence, Jeff developed schizophrenia, which gave him a dual mental health diagnosis. Schizophrenia is a very challenging condition by itself. It becomes even more challenging when combined with mental retardation. In addition to his intellectual disabilities, he had poor physical coordination to do the things most boys do, like ride a bike and play baseball. He was different, limited and often excluded.

Some people were mean to this calm, personable guy. Some were afraid and uncertain how to interact with Jeff because they were not knowledgeable about his condition. All they needed to do was smile and say hello. That's all he needed. He knew he was different. He knew who did and didn't like him. He knew he had limitations. How alone and unloved he must have felt. But still, he would shrug his shoulders and see the best in every situation by stating things like, "Well, at least I got to be here with everyone." Or, "I don't need a girlfriend when I got you, Sis," which of course, was my favorite line. The will and courage he showed more times than I can remember fill my heart with tears of pain and joy. After the difficulties of his childhood, of being different and not fitting into mainstream life, my beautiful Bro was accepted into a group-home living arrangement at the age of twenty-six. This was a great opportunity for him since he had lost his identity and sense of purpose during the five years since graduating from his high school. We all need an identity, a sense of purpose and belonging. Group-home living gave him his start on making his life better. He was becoming independent and happy with his achievements of being an assembly piece-worker, living away from home, losing a lot of weight and socializing with friends in his inspiring population. He was making his life sweeter! He was happy.

After a few years of success and happiness, Jeff had to face another hardship. At thirty-three, he was hit by a car as he crossed the street near his place of employment. Fortunately, the impact was not serious, but the emergency room misdiagnosis almost took his life. He was sent home to rest his leg. He formed a blood clot and had undetected trauma to his only kidney, which made him lethargic. He landed in the intensive care unit of a local hospital. When he was released, he went to a nursing home for six months of rehabilitation to his right knee and foot. This time was extremely depressing as he was placed with elderly people who were sick and dying--no place for a vibrant young man.

At this point in Jeff's life, we realized he would never have the opportunity to return to the glory and pride he had been feeling at his group home, because his new physical limitations would make him less independent. Since another one of Jeff's lemons was a diagnosis of renal disease for which there is no cure, he had knee replacement surgery at an earlier age than most recipients, to provide a better quality of life before eventually going on dialysis, receiving a kidney transplant or dying. The knee surgery was a tremendous success, and he was placed in a less independent group home where he found his new "other" family, which really was the best living arrangement he had had in his entire life. He really fit in there and had a true sense of belonging. Even though he would never get back to the peak of his independence, he was happy.

We became even closer as adults. We both said that we liked being "grown up" better. We had so much fun together and shared a deep, loving connection with our eyes that only we understood. He made my life sweeter. When my "Bro" peacefully took his final breaths in my arms two years ago, his gentle spirit moved into my soul forever. He is still helping me make peace, love and lemonade, and he always will.

I wrote the following poem about Jeff as a Christmas gift to our mother in 2001:

Does He Know?

He is the big, strong silent kind
That fills my heart and my mind

He has been sad; he has been mad
Yet, he has never been mean
Because his soul is calm
And his green eyes are so peaceful and serene

He is a grown man and he is a little boy
No matter who he is, he knows
The meaning of simple joy

He does not care for many books or jokes
Ah, but he has great stories and profound wit
That will amuse you if you give him a coax

People are afraid because they just don't know
They judge, they tease, they are unkind and he knows

He has experienced way too many hard times,
Endured so much hurt and pain
Yet, he continues to move forward in hope of
Acceptance to gain

Does he know how much his mother, his sister
And so many others love him?

He knows.

These two most influential people in my life have given me the courage, experiences and wisdom to help me really discover myself and evaluate my life. They have given me the inspiration and lessons needed to truly enjoy my time on earth. I know that loving people and living life are the greatest joys. My mother and brother showed me the way, by choosing to take all of their lemons and making the best lemonade ever. Now, you can understand why I was fortunate to have been born into inspiration.

When you reflect on the people who have influenced you most in your life, you can begin to understand who you are and who you have become. Appreciating and learning from these people, no matter how challenging or heartbreaking your experiences may have been, can't help but make your life sweeter.

CHAPTER 5:
SELF REFLECTION QUESTIONS

The following questions reflect the messages in this chapter. Answering them honestly will give you a greater understanding of how you may have evolved in your life and what you have learned from the people who have influenced your life. Remember, you have the power to make choices for yourself. You have the power to live a great life. You can choose to make lemonade.

Who has had the greatest influence on my life?

Who do I know that has made lemonade out of lemons? How did they do it?

What inspiration and lessons have I learned from them?

CHAPTER 6:
THE PEACE, LOVE AND LEMONADE INGREDIENTS

1/3 Accountability

1/3 Cup Attitude

1/3 Cup Action

In your moments of truth, are you embracing and living your life or are you just waking up each day existing in this world? Happiness is not just for some people; it is for all people. When you are deeply happy with who you are and who you have become, you feel pride within yourself for your efforts at discovering and doing. You realize that the hard work has helped you become more self-accepting and aware of yourself, others, and life's vast opportunities. You feel the natural highs that come from feeling alive, discovering new things, loving people and giving back to those in need. You are diggin' life.

Surely, sweet lemonade tastes better than sour, bitter lemons. Lemonade helps to satisfy your thirst for happiness

> When you are deeply happy with who you are and who you have become, you feel pride within yourself for your efforts at discovering and doing.

and peace, and the need to be loved and accepted. It gives you what you need to find your courage to love people and live life. When you choose to make lemonade from your lemons, your reactions to your tough circumstances will be motivating and your thinking will be optimistic. You will see your lemonade glass as half-full. You will begin nurturing yourself by applying your new skills and knowledge. Your positive results will inspire you when you begin deciding more times than not to make your life feel exhilarating.

It took me twenty to twenty-five years to unravel the first twenty years of my life. I made some choices that were good for me and some that were not. My actions made my experiences. Through organized and self-directed education and experiences, I discovered who I am. I healed my past and created a great way to live. I became who I am by the circumstances I experienced--both the good and the bad times. In each tough circumstance, I came to a point when I would say, "Enough is enough. I can't do this anymore! I can't take it anymore! I've had enough of feeling, living and working this way." Each time I reached my maxed-out limits, I would take ownership and become responsible for my life. Each time, I became accountable for my actions. Each time, I chose to make lemonade.

When you finally acknowledge that you are ready to make a change, embrace the "changing curve" with honesty, flexibility, patience, kindness, belief in yourself and belief in your desired outcomes. Admit your mistakes. If you are the type of person who is rigid or perhaps too idealistic and expects everything to go as planned, you will be setting yourself up for great frustrations and disappointments. Let it go and let it flow, baby!

1/3 CUP OF ACCOUNTABILITY

ACCOUNTABILITY →

THE 1ST INGREDIENT TO MEASURE
IS 1/3 CUP OF ACCOUNTABILITY.

....

*Add this by taking ownership for how
your actions and reactions affect yourself and others.*

Are you aware of what you want and need to change within you and your life to be happy and more fulfilled? Discovering these things is the very first step to making your life better. Becoming a person of accountability means that you have to acknowledge and take responsibility for your actions and reactions. If you think that you do not have any issues or limitations, think again. Everyone does. If you truly want to grow and enhance your life, *make the time* to be really honest with yourself. Even if it hurts you when you discover that you are not perfect and were wrong about something, realize what you need to change to grow and evolve.

If you stay sheltered and avoid the world's vast opportunities, you will never realize and understand the deeper essence of life. Life is so big that you really can't get it by living in your own world, mentally and physically. Living in a shallow, superficial world without much insight as to who you are and what's making you say and do the things you do will keep you unaware, which keeps you from growing. Becoming aware at conscious and deeper levels about yourself, others and your surroundings will bring you an abundance of openness and varying perspectives that are essential ingredients for making peace, love and lemonade. You need to keep your eyes open and your mind aware of the choices you have when you are ready to get happy. Accountability requires change.

Change is a difficult process; so many people resist it with a vengeance. It's hard mostly because it takes time and involves loss. Something must be given up or taken away, and the situation will no longer feel comfortable, easy or safe in the way it once did. Our fast-paced society leads people to expect quick fixes and instant gratification.

Become open to examining how you act and react. Learn to think long-term, not short-term. It's like delegating a chore at home or a task at work. Many people do not delegate because they think it is quicker to complete the task themselves instead of taking the time to educate, train and monitor someone else's completion of the task. Sure this is a quick short-term fix, but does it really free up your time in the long-term? When you decide to take on something that you know you can and could delegate, does something inside tell you that you really can't and that you shouldn't be the one completing the task? Chances are that was your intuition, a.k.a. your gut. Your gut was telling you the truth, the right thing to do. Have you ever had the sharp pain in your gut when you read or heard something that you knew was true about yourself, and it was not such a great trait? The awareness of your flaw hurt, didn't it? The feeling of hurt in your gut was a clue for you to look more closely into the message. The pain that you surely would prefer to avoid makes you transform and grow. When you acknowledge, accept and own your problems and limitations, you take control of your life through accountability.

My estranged father was not a man of accountability. A day before my thirty-ninth birthday, I received a totally unexpected call from him. Life can creep up and make us remember, reflect and feel those things we've been avoiding and burying inside our souls. My father, who was on dialysis, said he wanted to wish me happy birthday and rekindle our relationship, which had been pretty much nonexistent my entire life. I honestly believe he thought I was born on April 4th and not my actual, grateful day of being brought into this world on April 5th. He had never popped into my life on my actual birthday. He was a father who would come in and out of my life when it was convenient for him, on the odd occasion he remembered that he had a kid.

Over the years, I had made attempts to have a relationship with him and to understand his side of the story. Each time, he would change the subject, and I would leave disappointed and discouraged. He did not take responsibility for the two children he brought into this world; for more than forty years he chose not to make peace, love and lemonade for himself or his family. Since I had tried to make contact with him on many occasions over the years, I thought my father was a little too late to begin the journey of building a relationship--especially since he did not make the attempt before he was dying and feeling regrets.

He was my father through biology, not through life. I had a hard time addressing him as "Dad," since he really wasn't one. I always felt awkward in those moments, so I simply omitted the acknowledgement. During that pre-birthday phone call, I recall saying, "I'm sorry you're not doing well. I wish the best for you. I'm okay now, doing good, and I don't feel the need to rekindle any kind of relationship with you. Take care." Whoa, was that powerful for me!

I cried and released a lot of pent-up hurt and disappointment. This emotional release helped me to heal another buried wound. How empowering and wonderful I felt that I was now strong enough to take control of how I was going to live my life and let go of this baggage. I shared this with a friend and told her, "The next time I see him will be at the funeral."

She asked, "Whose funeral?"

I replied, "His." Shockingly, we both laughed. Not at him

or his dying.   We laughed at finding humor in the harsh reality
of the situation.   My harsh reality was my finally accepting that
I would never have the father-daughter relationship I always
wanted. I thought that old remote chapter and its negative hold
on my life was over.   It was not.

Three years later, I received the call that my father had been
life-flighted to a Cleveland hospital after a massive heart attack.
He was not expected to make it. I felt the need to go see him
while he was in a coma and drove the two hours to Cleveland
from Pittsburgh. I honestly thought I was done crying, grieving
and healing over my father. No way. I really crashed hard for
three days, full of tears from the deep pain and anger I still had
buried within me from his abandoning me and my family.   I
guess since death is so real and raw, my deepest emotions were
finally being released.

When I walked into his hospital room, the most amazing
thing occurred. There was no pain, there was no anger, there
was no history; there was only compassion for a human being.
I saw a man who could not help himself with his life
circumstances--a man who chose not to make his life better. A
man whose time on earth was done. I knew this man could
never get his act together for himself or his family. He twitched
when I spoke. Perhaps he recognized my voice, and perhaps he
did not.   I said, "Dad, it's me, Nancy. I came up from
Pittsburgh. Jeff and I are okay now. It's okay to let go and find
peace. I love you. See ya." It was natural, and it was loving. I

even called him "Dad."

My father is at peace and so am I. I am not certain if my mother has peace yet. I do know she had compassion for me when I told her the story. She knew about my heartache from years of searching and hoping for a relationship with my father that was never going to happen. I remember walking into her kitchen and telling her what had happened. I can still see her compassionate expression for me over a man who had made her life extremely painful and hard. She was mostly concerned about my reaction to his death and my well-being. She responded with a kind softness and said, "Did he die?"

So you see, my father played a significant role in my life even though he was not physically near. The results of my father's continuous abandonment were deep within me. I had a shame seed that had not yet been removed. It made me believe that I was not deserving of love. I wasn't even aware of the source of shame. Sometimes it takes years to understand the significance of a situation. Once you become self-aware, you can start to become accountable for your actions. You must take ownership of whatever you need to change. When you stay in denial about how you influence your own experiences, you do not grow. More importantly, when you do not accept how you contribute to the unhappiness in your life and in the lives of others, nothing will change. To fully embrace life, choose to become a person of accountability. It's a critical ingredient you need to add to your lemonade.

My 1/3 Cup of Accountability Worksheet

Use the following questions on the next page to begin the process of taking ownership for how your actions and reactions affect yourself and others. Reflect on the lemon you selected previously. Realize what's working for you and what is not. Write your responses to discover how you are about to become accountable.

CHAPTER 6:
MY 1/3 CUP OF ACCOUNTABILITY WORKSHEET

What Do I Need to Become Accountable For?	My 1/3 Cup of Accountability Responses
Why do I want to become accountable and make changes in my life?	
What do I already do now that brings me positive results?	
How do these positive ways of acting and reacting affect me and the others involved?	
What do I do that brings me negative results?	
How do these negative ways of acting and reacting affect me and the others involved?	
What are my desired ways of acting and reacting?	

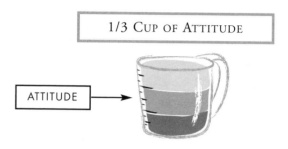

1/3 CUP OF ATTITUDE

ATTITUDE →

THE 2ND INGREDIENT TO MEASURE
IS 1/3 CUP OF ATTITUDE.

....

*Add this by changing your negative thoughts and
beliefs into positive thoughts and beliefs.*

The energy-boosting ingredient to make the best lemonade
ever is one-third cup attitude. Our attitude tells us whether we
can or cannot achieve something and whether we believe or do
not believe in ourselves. Most importantly, our attitude drives
us to want or not want to get out of our comfort zones to make
positive changes in our lives. Many have said, "We can do
anything we *want* to," or "Where there's a will there's a way."
Belief in yourself is the power behind success.

We may desire many things in our lives but do not take
action to obtain them. If we do not take action, perhaps way
down in our unconscious, some buried negative thoughts are
keeping us from wanting our goals badly enough to pursue
them actively. Since your core thoughts come before your

actions, you let them decide first whether or not you will make your dreams come true.

Belief in yourself is the power behind success.

Your thoughts determine the attitudes you carry and the ways you live your life. If you keep thinking negative thoughts about yourself, others and the world, you will take negative actions that lead to negative results. On the flipside, if you keep thinking positive thoughts about yourself, others and the world, you will take positive actions that will lead to positive results. Only when you are really ready, really sick and tired of how you feel day in and day out, will you start doing something about it. Perhaps you may say to yourself: "I'm sick of worrying and being unhappy." In your lowest moments, begin to think and says things differently like, "I really want to be happy." This is when the magic occurs. When you catch yourself thinking negative thoughts, stop and change your inner dialogue. Slowly but surely, you become happy because you begin doing things differently, thus getting different results. You begin discovering your very own refreshing positive thoughts. You begin thinking optimistically and doing things that make you feel happy. A smile, a laugh, and a check mark on your "to-do" list are contagious and continuously breed success, happiness and confidence. You finally begin to believe that your life can be different; you believe in yourself. You have evolved into happiness by choosing the power of positive thinking. You have found hope.

On a typical 3H (hazy, hot and humid) summer afternoon in Pittsburgh, I gazed out my bedroom window singing the lyrics to my favorite George Benson rendition of the song, "*The Greatest Love of All*":

I DECIDED LONG AGO, NEVER TO
WALK IN ANYONE'S SHADOWS
IF I FAIL, IF I SUCCEED
AT LEAST I LIVE AS I BELIEVE
NO MATTER WHAT THEY TAKE FROM ME
THEY CAN'T TAKE AWAY MY DIGNITY
BECAUSE THE GREATEST LOVE OF ALL
IS HAPPENING TO ME
I FOUND THE GREATEST LOVE OF ALL
INSIDE OF ME

I loved the music with George's soulful voice and the lyrics. I would sing with him (very off-key, I confess) with great passion, pain and hope. It took me almost thirty years actually to believe the words deep in both my heart and my mind. Like any teenager, I thought I knew it all when I was acting out in my rebellious teen years. I definitely did not know about instilling love within me back then, but now I finally do. The writer of this song, Linda Creed, knew all along about where to find the "greatest love of all." It was within my own heart, within my own beliefs about myself. Find your "greatest love of all." Find hope.

I recall my bedroom window as being the place where I found hope. It was where I would say to myself, "Things are going to be better for me when I get out on my own." I remember the many times I leaned out my bedroom window, which was part of our half of the duplex we rented. I shared one of the three small bedrooms with my mother. She had one twin bed. I had the other. Imagine a teenage girl who hated herself, her life and of course her mother, just like many teenage girls do, sleeping each night only a foot away from her mother. At that time, I really wanted my own space and a place to stash my weed and smokes. Our low income could not afford it. My ungrateful self would not let me see that at least I finally had my own bed after many years of our sharing just one with my mother and brother. More importantly, I couldn't realize that having my mother near did provide me with the security of knowing I was safe and loved each night. The experience of sharing a bedroom with my mother brought about in its own peculiar way what I needed most at that time--to feel safe and loved. We all need to feel safe and loved.

While George's wonderful rendition still deeply touches my soul every time I hear it, I now find Louis Armstrong's song "Wonderful World" resonating more, simply because it is indeed a wonderful world. My transformation throughout this wonderful world began many years ago, with singing out my bedroom window where I was finding hope and dreaming of a better life. I was aware that other people were happy and living differently than I was. I knew that there were other people in the world who had it better than I and that someday, without knowing when or how, I was going to make a better life for myself. I would have my own bedroom where I would wake up each morning, feeling exhilarated, singing Louis' song: "I see trees of green…red roses too; I see 'em bloom…for me and for you; and I think to myself…what a wonderful world." At the end of each day, I fall into my slumbers calmly singing my new version of George's rendition: "If I failed, if I succeeded today, at least I lived as I believed." The power of my hope and attitude brought me to this fabulous point in my life. If thirty years ago, I had looked out my bedroom window without finding hope, I wouldn't be sitting here writing this book and diggin' life.

Realize and believe that your life can be better as you groove through life's ups and downs. Repeatedly tell yourself that things will get better--even during your lowest moments when you truly believe they won't. This is called hope. Realize that circumstances eventually change. You might feel low, and think of the worst case scenarios during your melt-down moments. It's okay; meltdowns happen. Just remember that life does get better when you believe in yourself and have hope.

> Repeatedly tell yourself that things will get better -- even during your lowest moments when you truly believe they won't.

My 1/3 Cup of Attitude Worksheet

Use the following questions to begin the process of changing your negative thoughts into positive ones. Reflect on the lemon you selected previously. Write your responses to discover how positive you already are and how much more positive you *could* become. Question seven, will require you to repeat your new positive affirmations. With practice, your affirmations can become ingrained in your positive thinking system.

CHAPTER 6:
MY 1/3 CUP OF ATTITUDE WORKSHEET

What am I Thinking?	My 1/3 Cup of Attitude Responses
What are my positive thoughts about myself, my life and others in my life?	
What are the facts that show they are true?	
Where did my positive thoughts come from?	
What are my negative thoughts about myself, my life and others in my life? What are the facts that show they are true?	
Where did my negative thoughts come from?	
What three affirmations will I continuously say to myself when I start to think negative thoughts? Create a separate affirmation for each negative thought you experience.	1. 2. 3.

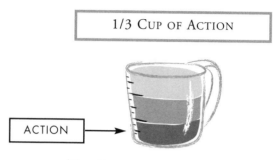

1/3 CUP OF ACTION

ACTION

THE 3RD INGREDIENT TO MEASURE
IS 1/3 CUP OF ACTION.

....

Add this by taking initiative and starting to do something.

Once you become honestly aware of the challenging areas in both your personal and professional lives, you will know what to change and you will be ready to add the final necessary lemonade ingredient: one-third cup of action. When you think differently and choose to do something different, you act differently and get different results. Your life will remain the same if you do not change your patterns of thought and behavior. If you do not take action, your life will not change. Your problems will not go away.

Being surrounded by intellectual conversations about politics, history or religion at family gatherings was very intimidating for me. I had no confidence and very little knowledge of the subject matters, especially when others used "big words." I did not have a large vocabulary and would sit in silence around the table, not willing to add to the conversation. I felt very inadequate. I was a life-smart kid, not a book-smart kid. For many years, at family gatherings and work meetings, I would freeze around the meeting table. I felt great pressure to speak up in a way that would not sound "stupid."

At one point in my career, I was asked to attend a meeting with the senior management team. What an honor. What pressure. Well guess what? I became frozen in my fear and could not speak. I failed just like I did when I was that little girl on the nursery school stage. Fortunately, one of the executives pulled me aside afterwards and said, "Nancy, you just have to blurt it out in this group. You were asked here for your expertise. Share it."

His words gave me both permission and confidence to speak. Even though he spoke with me, I was never asked back to join the senior management team meetings. I had blown it again! For a while, I can recall sitting in many meetings feeling intense angst and pressure to speak up because all eyes were upon me. I knew I had to try. I couldn't realistically expect to get different results if I didn't do something different. I had to utilize my power of choice.

Each time I spoke, each time I achieved a mini success, I reduced my fear and built my confidence. "Wow, I actually had a few smarts, and I helped!" With effort and practice, I hardly

> **Persevere and do not give up too soon or you will miss out on the opportunity to transform and grow.**

feel any angst in meetings or family gatherings. Thank goodness. By deciding to take action, I utilized my power of choice. I made my work life and my personal life sweeter. Had I not decided to take action, I would have been sitting there beating myself up and dreading each meeting or family gathering.

To this day, I still do not have a large vocabulary and at times, I have to ask people what some of their words mean. Oh, well. When we take a car trip to a new destination for the first time, the ride there seems to take forever. We may even get lost and have to ask for directions. Then on the ride home, the ride seems much quicker because we are more familiar with the route. We had a practice ride so we didn't get lost again. As Ralph Waldo Emerson said, "Unless you try to do something beyond what you've already mastered, you will never grow."

Repetitive practice and actions are necessary for success. You cannot realistically expect to become the master of anything the first time around, nor will it happen the second or third. Persevere and do not give up too soon or you will miss out on the opportunity to transform and grow.

People who are involved with life and are working in high-level professions have put forth quite a bit of hard work and effort to reach their achievements. New knowledge gives them tremendous understanding and expansion into many interesting arenas for their personal and professional lives. Most importantly, they do not leave their knowledge and understanding in their brains--they apply them. Experiencing new people, activities, jobs and asking questions helps to keep your mind stimulated and your life lively. If, on the other hand, you choose to maintain friendships with only the same kind of people, and employment in the same industry and levels, you will be left with fewer opportunities to broaden your horizons. You could end up doing the same things, which can bring you complacency.

You can learn and become rich about many things from the many different kinds of people you meet and experiences you embrace. Most importantly, you reduce your worrying when you become aware and gain new knowledge. By knowing and experiencing many diverse people and ways of living, you have less fear of the unknown because you are making choices based on your knowledge and understanding. Your inflexible, rigid nature will diminish when you open your mind. When you take the initiative to gain new knowledge and become open to different perspectives, you can calm your fears and find easier ways to react to the world and people around you.

My 1/3 Cup of Action Plan Worksheet

Use the following questions to begin the process of taking action. Determine what has greater value to you: the rewards for taking action or the consequences for not taking action. Reflect on the lemon you selected previously. Write your responses to make your plan of action. Make a commitment to yourself to take initiative and practice continuously. Toot your horn and celebrate your successes!

CHAPTER 6:
MY 1/3 CUP OF ACTION PLAN WORKSHEET

What are My Successes and Goals?	My 1/3 Cup of Action Plan Responses
What successful experiences am I most proud of because of how I handled them?	
What did I specifically do that contributed to my success?	
Of the things I now want to change in my life, what action do I need to take?	
What will be the rewards if I decide to take action?	
What will be the consequences if I decide not to take action?	
What are my desired ways of acting and reacting?	
How can I make sure that I will do something different this time?	

WHICH WOULD YOU PREFER?

CHAPTER 6:
SELF REFLECTION QUESTIONS

The following questions reflect the messages in this chapter. Answer them honestly and decide whether you want to make yourself happier and your life more fulfilling. If your answers to the following questions are mostly "yes" or "often," it's time to consider making some positive changes in your life. Remember, you have the power to make choices for yourself. You have the power to live a great life. You can choose to make lemonade.

In my moment of truth, am I just waking up each day feeling stuck and existing in this world?

Do I have difficulty admitting my mistakes and becoming accountable for how my actions and reactions affect my life and the lives of others?

Do I wish I had back the time and energy I spent trying to fix the same mistakes?

Do I seek short-term fixes to problems and challenges?

Do I honestly react with a "can't-do" attitude?

Do I have a difficult time believing in myself?

Do I accept the status quo and let things remain as they are?

Do I stay sheltered by not exploring new people, places and things to broaden my horizons?

Have I stopped learning and practicing to master my talents and abilities?

Do I struggle with tooting my own horn and acknowledging my successes?

CHAPTER 7:
THE PURPOSE OF TOUGH TIMES

Our challenging experiences help us learn lessons about life. The lessons of life help us to grow if we choose to apply them in our lives. They teach us what to do and not to do the next time we encounter a similar situation. Doing something positive the next time determines whether or not we actually learned the lessons.

Do we have to have hardships and tragedies in our lives to make our lives sweeter? While some people wait until someone close to them is on his or her death bed to express their love, others completely miss out on the caring, wonderful moments. They wish they could have spent more time together. Others wait until something goes wrong with their health to start taking better care of themselves. Many others spend forty hours or more of their week working in a job that brings them only negative energy and dread each day. Many people stay in dead-end relationships that exhaust them and make them unhappy. These folks never give themselves the opportunity to meet their true Mr. or Mrs. Right. It seems to be a human tendency to wait until a situation is no longer tolerable or a tremendous consequence is experienced before people choose to do something different--to make a change. This human tendency makes many people reactive instead of proactive in their approaches to people and situations. Their deeper thoughts about what they think they deserve, the ways

> **Tough times can build your strength and character if you decide to embrace instead of resist them.**

they take people and life for granted, and how they continually choose to take the path of least resistance take precedence. Make peace, love and lemonade before you no longer can. It's never too late to get happy.

Whether you go through tough times due to being reactive or proactive, doesn't matter as much as choosing to learn and do something positive from your circumstances. There is much strength and wisdom to be gained from tough times. When you go through tough times, you can bounce back stronger and develop greater character if you choose to do something positive. Challenging times enhance your life by helping you grow. Your life experiences bring you understanding and insights so you can respond more effectively to the world around you.

When you experience difficult times and tragedies, you can become more resilient, more empathic and eventually, more likely to be happy. Tough times can build your strength and character if you decide to embrace instead of resist them. Through your hurts and disappointments, you can discover the preciousness of life. You can stop taking people and life for granted. You can also discover the magic of living generously by sharing your lemonade with others. You can give back your courage, assertiveness and passion by helping people realize that they too can get through their hard times. You can give your strength, wisdom and lessons learned to others. The abundant cycle of making lemonade out of lemons continues. People will benefit tremendously from your kindness and compassion.

When you realize that your difficult times are lessons to help you learn and grow, by reflecting, discovering and doing something good with them, you are making everyone's life easier. Many of the circumstances you experience can be tough, but they almost always lead to opportunities for greater growth. For example, my mother wanted to be a stay-at-home mom. This would have been wonderful for her if her circumstances had been right; however, they weren't. She saw no choice but to improve the situation. She persevered in starting a long journey for herself and her two children, from welfare to earning her law degree. With each step of courage and determination, she reached another height of achievement. With each achievement and setback, she had more strength and hope. Now, that's a sweeter

A tough situation can be an opportunity.

life; that's lemonade!

A tough situation can be an opportunity. You have to become fully aware at a conscious level to see the opportunity. When you choose to make things better for yourself, you will be aware of why you are responding to situations and people as you do. For example, until my father's death, I was not aware of the deep-down shame that I was holding in about his abandonment of my family and me. I felt there had to be something wrong with me for him not to want me. Consequently, I made poor choices because I didn't think I was worthy of happiness. I know the opportunity was there all along. I just didn't see it. I did not consciously realize that I needed to find peace through forgiving my estranged father and being kind to myself. Oh, the lessons, truths and opportunities our experiences can bring us if we just embrace them.

If your experiences are minimal, then your deeper understanding of people and life are minimal. When you don't expose yourself to new experiences, you're playing it safe by not exploring and venturing into a fuller life and a deeper understanding. You may or may not be the only person responsible for bringing about your tough circumstances. But, you definitely are the only one responsible for how you react to them.

"Carondo, Carondo, Wanna. Ugh. Carondo, Carondo,

Wanna, ugh. We like Carondo Wanna, you like Carondo Wanna, ugh, ugh, ugh!" Life doesn't get any better than when I reflect back to my favorite childhood memory of singing this chant at the YWCA Camp Carondowanna during the summer of 1973.

During the summer after I completed the sixth grade, I experienced my first time away from home without any family. I had the time of my life, getting up at the crack of dawn and walking across the morning-dewed grass to hang the American flag in my pajamas. I would sing this chant while sitting around the campfire with my newfound family; I felt my first real sense of belonging by bonding with the counselors and my camper friends. The beauty and peace of nature have always lifted my spirits and calmed me. I was part of something where everything and everyone were connected. I felt wanted. I cherished that time. I liked it so much that I later applied to be a camp counselor as my summer job.

I wanted to feel those good feelings of belonging again. I wanted that sense of being wanted and accepted. I wanted to relive what I did not have while I was living at home. I wanted to go backward instead of forward. However, anywhere I applied for a camp counselor summer job, I was rejected. Once again, I thought that I wasn't good enough. I failed and could not go back to that place and feeling that I really wanted.

For some reason, I also applied for a summer job at an amusement park in Ohio. I was, much to my surprise, scheduled for an interview with a recruiter who was coming to my college campus. I got the job but didn't know for what position. At that point, it didn't matter to me because I just wanted to get away from my hometown. When I received my job assignment information, I discovered that I had been placed in the amusement park's games department--not the rides, not the food stands, but the games, which required an outgoing personality. Shy, introverted me? Never.

Well, I guess there must be some truth to the Rolling Stones lyrics to "Satisfaction": "We can't always get what we want, but if we try some time, we just might find we get what we need." In an introspective moment twenty-five years later, I realized why I did not get a camp counselor job. It was not what I needed. It was just what I wanted. Meanwhile, the amusement park employment office thought the games position was the best fit for me. I *needed* to go forward, not backward to make my life better. I *needed* to work as a games hostess, a.k.a. "carnie."

My true career calling is to be a public speaker and trainer, and my amusement park job was exactly what I needed to get me on my way to making my career happen. At that time, I did not understand my deeper reasoning for wanting to be a camp counselor. I was making a decision based on reasoning that could have been detrimental to my pursuit of happiness. Thank goodness the people reviewing the applications realized that I was not meant to be a camp counselor. I needed to get out of my introverted self and start belting out with confidence and enthusiasm: "TWENTY-FIVE CENTS TO PLAY, TWENTY-FIVE CENTS TO WIN, COME ON IN!" not "Carondo, Carondo, Wanna, ugh." A camp counselor job would have made me feel good at the time, but would have kept me from becoming what I am meant to be. I might have become stuck and not as happy as I could be.

These opposite spectrums taught me how sometimes we are not able to see for ourselves what is best for us. When things do not happen as we had hoped, we just may end up better off--with something other than what we thought we wanted. We can usually end up with what we really need instead.

I still wonder what I said or did that made the recruiter believe I was a good fit for the games department. I guess he saw something in me that I didn't. I guess he knew what Mick Jagger sang about: let me give this young woman what she needs to blossom out of her shell into her full greatness potential, an opportunity to have something good happen in her life, a chance to build her confidence, overcome her fears and find her true calling. I have learned that we cannot get what we want until we first get what we need. While differentiating between our wants and needs can be tricky, determining our core needs can help us eventually to get what we want.

Two people can perceive things so differently. The two people who influenced my life the most had different thoughts about why I decided to leave home for the first time. After I was living away from my family for a few years, I was chatting with my mother and brother about why I left home. My brother's opinion was that "I *needed* to do my own thing," and my mother's opinion was that "I *needed* to get the hell out of here." They were both right.

I *needed* to do both, to explore other ways of living and to get away from the situations that were making me unhappy. I didn't *want* to stay stuck. I *wanted* to be happy. I didn't know how to make myself happy and my life more fulfilling. I do now. Are you ready to make yourself happy and your life more fulfilling?

You can overcome life's challenges. You can utilize your power of choice when you experience tough times. You now know how to make lemonade out of your lemons. Being born into inspiration is how I started my book, my story. My story reveals how my family and I experienced many difficult and painful times. My story also boasts about how each of us turned ourselves around and made our lives sweeter. My story will continue, and I now know that it will have a happy ending. We all have a story. What's your story? How did it begin? More importantly, how will your story end?

Go confidently in the direction of your dreams!

Live the life you've imagined.

-- Henry David Thoreau

THE FOLLOWING PAGES

CONTAIN ADDITIONAL

WORKSHEETS TO ASSIST

YOU IN MAKING YOUR

LIFE SWEETER.

Gathering My Lemons	My Lemon Reflections
What lemons have I experienced in my life?	
Which lemon is still bringing me difficulties?	
Which one will I gather?	
At the time when I got handed this lemon, why did I think it happened?	
What impact did the difficult experience have on me and those who were involved?	
Reflecting back, now, why do I think I was handed this lemon and what did I learn from this tough time?	

What Seeds are in My Lemon?	My Lemon Seed Responses
What am I angry about with regard to my lemon? Why? How can I forgive myself and others, and appreciate the lemon?	
What do I feel guilty about with regard to my lemon? How can I forgive myself and others, and appreciate the lemon?	
What am I ashamed of with regard to my lemon? Why? How can I forgive myself and others, and appreciate the lemon?	
What can I start feeling lighthearted about with regard to my lemon? Why? How can I learn to appreciate lightheartedness?	
In general what can I do to become more lighthearted in my life?	

Assertiveness Questions	My Assertiveness Applied
What is the situation I want to handle assertively?	
What is my desired outcome of this situation?	
What is keeping me from being assertive?	
What do I need to say, think and do differently?	
What are the consequences if I don't handle this situation assertively?	
What are the rewards if I do handle this situation assertively?	
Each night before I fall asleep and each morning as soon as I wake up, I will say to myself ten times, "I am assertive and courageous."	
Each day, I will take a 15-minute "me-time" break to do what?	

I Am Passionate! Worksheet

Passion Questions	My Passion Applied
What are some things that I have liked doing in the past and currently enjoy doing? 1. 2. 3. 4. 5.	What are some things that I have liked doing in the past and currently absolutely love doing? 1. 2. 3. 4. 5.
What are some things that I really miss doing? 1. 2. 3. 4. 5.	What are some the things that I always wanted to do in my lifetime? 1. 2. 3. 4. 5.
What are some activities that I no longer need in my life? 1. 2. 3.	From the lists above, what acitivty(ies) will I bring into my life? 1. 2. 3.

What Do I Need to Become Accountable For?	My 1/3 Cup of Accountability Responses
Why do I want to become accountable and make changes in my life?	
What do I already do now that brings me positive results?	
How do these positive ways of acting and reacting affect me and the others involved?	
What do I do that brings me negative results?	
How do these negative ways of acting and reacting affect me and the others involved?	
What are my desired ways of acting and reacting?	

My 1/3 Cup of Attitude Worksheet

What am I Thinking?	My 1/3 Cup of Attitude Responses
What are my positive thoughts about myself, my life and others in my life?	
What are the facts that show they are true?	
Where did my positive thoughts come from?	
What are my negative thoughts about myself, my life and others in my life?	
What are the facts that show they are true?	
Where did my negative thoughts come from?	
What three affirmations will I continuously say to myself when I start to think negative thoughts? Create a separate affirmation for each negative thought you experience.	1. 2. 3.

MY 1/3 CUP OF ACTION PLAN WORKSHEET

What are My Successes and Goals?	My 1/3 Cup of Action Plan Responses
What successful experiences am I most proud of because of how I handled them?	
What did I specifically do that contributed to my success?	
Of the things I now want to change in my life, what action do I need to take?	
What will be the rewards if I decide to take action?	
What will be the consequences if I decide not to take action?	
What are my desired ways of acting and reacting?	
How can I make sure that I will do something different this time?	

NOTES AND REFLECTIONS

NOTES AND REFLECTIONS

Personal Growth Reading Nancy Has Enjoyed

Burns, David D. M.D.
Feeling Good: The New Mood Therapy
New York: Avon Books, 1980

Goleman, Daniel
Emotional Intelligence: Why it Can Matter More than IQ.
New York: Bantam Books, 1995

Kasl, Charlotte. Ph.D.
If the Buddha Dated:
A Handbook for Finding Love on a Spiritual Path
New York: Penguin Group, 1999

Katie, Byron.
Loving What Is.
New York: Harmony Books, 2002.

McGraw, Phillip C., Ph.D.
Self Matters: Creating Your Life from the Inside Out
New York: Simon & Schuster Source, 2001

Ruiz, Don Miguel
The Four Agreements: A Practical Guide to Personal Freedom.
San Rafael, California: Amber-Allen Publishing, 1997

Simon, Sidney B. M.D., and Simon, Suzanne
Forgiveness: How to Make Peace with Your
Past and Get on With Your Life
New York: Warner Books, 1990

Whitfield, Charles L. M.D.
Healing the Child Within: Discovery and Recovery for Adult
Children of Dysfunctional Families
Deerfield Beach, FL: Health Communications, Inc., 1987

Willard, Robert F., Ph.D. Gibertini, Michael Ph.D.
The Seven Jewels of Codependency
Canada: 7JOC Press, 2002

About Nancy and Silver Lining Solutions™

She's passionate. She practices what she speaks and writes. And true to her company's name, she believes in silver linings and the possibilities found in every day.

Nancy Stampahar, founder of Silver Lining Solutions™, is a resilient individual whose life experiences have shaped her into a wellspring of positive energy, compassion and achievement. She has found her calling to help people discover the abundance of opportunities within themselves and in the world around them.

She believes that a powerful impact can occur when people combine their "can-do, will-do" attitudes, skills and knowledge with goal-setting and development activities, because an empowered individual moves companies and lives, which in turn, sets positive change in motion in the world.

Silver Lining Solutions™ is a professional development training and keynote speaking business. It is known for customizing each organizational training workshop and public speaking engagement. Nancy is known for engaging audiences and inspiring them to take action. Let Silver Lining Solutions™ help you achieve results through interactive learning, thinking and fun!

Some of Nancy's Achievements

- Backed by over a decade of leadership and training experiences in more than 20 different performance improvement methods, she improved performances in the academic, healthcare, non-profit, retail, travel and tourism, manufacturing, telecommunications and technology industries.

- Held employment positions that developed diverse business skills in customer service, general operations management, human resources, organizational development, and sales in various parts of the country.

- Has given extensive time to not-for-profit organizations during most of her life and has recently created "The Over 21 Disabilities Project," a fundraising initiative.

To discover more, please visit silverliningsolutions.com and peaceloveandlemonade.com.

To schedule Nancy, contact info@silverliningsolutions.com.

Dear Reader,

In celebration of my brother, Jeff, and his inspiring friends, I created "The Over 21 Disabilities Project," which is a fundraising initiative. I am raising money because there are over 22,000 people with disabilities on the Pennsylvania statewide wait list who need various community and support services as soon as they turn 21.

To learn more about this increasing crisis, please visit: pawaitinglistcampaign.org.

A portion of my book's proceeds will go to The Jeffrey J. Stampahar Fund at ACHIEVA. Jeff's restricted fund will specifically support advocacy costs related to reducing the community and support services waitlists for people with mental health/mental retardation disabilities who are over 21 years of age.

To learn more about the not-for-profit organization, ACHIEVA, who is the provider of these advocacy efforts and the recipient of the monies, please visit: achieva.info.

continued on next page >

If you would like to make a donation,
please make your check payable to:

"The Jeffrey J. Stampahar Fund at ACHIEVA."

Mail to:
ACHIEVA, Director of Development
711 Bingham Street
Pittsburgh, PA 15203-1007

Or, you can make an on-line donation at:
peaceloveandlemonade.com.
Thank you for your compassion and support.

Wishing you peace, love and lemonade,
Nancy Stampahar